Impressionist to Early Modern Paintings from the U.S.S.R.

Impressionist to Early Modern Paintings from the U.S.S.R.

Works from The Hermitage Museum, Leningrad, and The Pushkin Museum of Fine Arts, Moscow

National Gallery of Art, Washington

Los Angeles County Museum of Art, Los Angeles

The Metropolitan Museum of Art, New York

Occidental Petroleum Corporation
and The Armand Hammer Foundation, Los Angeles

Edited and designed by The Armand Hammer Foundation in conjunction with Harry N. Abrams, Inc., Publishers, New York.

This exhibition is made possible through the cooperation of the Ministry of Culture of the U.S.S.R.; the Hermitage Museum, Leningrad; the Pushkin Museum of Fine Arts, Moscow; the National Gallery of Art, Washington, D.C.; the Los Angeles County Museum of Art; The Metropolitan Museum of Art, New York; and The Armand Hammer Foundation, Los Angeles.

Major funding is provided by Occidental Petroleum Corporation, Los Angeles.

The exchange of exhibitions between the Soviet Union and the United States is supported by an indemnity from the Federal Council on the Arts and the Humanities.

Paintings are reproduced with permission from the Ministry of Culture of the U.S.S.R.

Library of Congress Cataloging-in-Publication Data

Impressionist to early modern paintings from the U.S.S.R.

"Works from the Hermitage Museum, Leningrad, and the Pushkin Museum of Fine Arts, Moscow."
Exhibition catalog.
Bibliography: p.
1. Impressionism (Art)—French—Exhibitions. 2. Post-impressionism—France—Exhibitions. 3. Painting, French—Exhibitions. 4. Painting, Modern—19th century—France—Exhibitions. 5. Gosudarstvennyĭ Ermitazh (Soviet Union) 6. Gosudarstvennyĭ muzeĭ izobrazitel'nykh iskusstv imeni A.S. Puchkina—Exhibitions. I. Gosudarstvennyĭ Ermitazh (Soviet Union) II. Gosudarstvennyĭ muzeĭ izobrazitelńykh iskusstv imeni A.S. Puchkina. III. Occidental Petroleum Corporation. IV. Armand Hammer Foundation.
ND547.5.I5I467 1986   759.4'074'013   86–7251

No part of this publication may be reproduced without written permission from The Armand Hammer Foundation.

Cover: Matisse, *Goldfish*, 1911 (cat. no. 29)
Page 6: Photo by Bill Fitz-Patrick, courtesy of The White House, Washington, D.C.

This catalogue accompanies the exhibition *Impressionist to Early Modern Paintings from the U.S.S.R.* The text was coordinated by The Armand Hammer Foundation from Soviet and American sources.

The introduction, catalogue entries, and bibliography and exhibitions section were prepared by A.G. Kostenevich for the Hermitage Museum and Marina Bessonova for the Pushkin Museum of Fine Arts. These texts were provided primarily in Russian and were translated and edited for this catalogue.

The artists' biographies are adapted from biographies that appeared originally in *Impressionist and Post-Impressionist Paintings from the U.S.S.R.*, M. Knoedler and Co., Inc., New York, 1973.

Titles of paintings are those used in the catalogue raisonné or other standard English language reference for each work.

Printed and bound in the United States of America.

Contents

Letter from Ronald Reagan
President of the United States   7

Preface by Armand Hammer   8

Foreword by J. Carter Brown, Earl A. Powell III,
and Philippe de Montebello   9

Introduction by A. Kostenevich and M. Bessonova   12

List of Plates   24

Catalogue   27

Selected Bibliography and Exhibitions   123

George P. Shultz, U.S. Secretary of State, and Eduard A. Shevardnadze, Foreign Minister of the U.S.S.R., signing the cultural agreement at the Geneva Summit, November 1985, with Ronald Reagan and Mikhail Gorbachev looking on.

THE WHITE HOUSE
WASHINGTON

March 11, 1986

I am delighted to extend my congratulations and very best wishes on the occasion of this exhibition -- a truly significant cultural event between the United States and the Soviet Union. An exchange of masterpieces with the renowned Hermitage and Pushkin Museums is a most fitting way to inaugurate the agreement General Secretary Gorbachev and I concluded in Geneva to expand the cultural and artistic relations between our two countries.

As a result of this exchange, Americans during 1986 will have an exceptional opportunity to enjoy in Washington, D.C., Los Angeles and New York City a magnificent group of Impressionist and Post-Impressionist masterworks from collections in the Soviet Union. I am most pleased that Soviet citizens also will be able to enjoy in Leningrad and Moscow superlative American exhibitions from the National Gallery of Art and the Armand Hammer Foundation.

The fine arts provide a unique avenue for promoting greater understanding and for appreciating the truth that men and women everywhere are bound together by hopes and dreams that transcend national boundaries. Our debt to artists of genius is immense; we can repay it, if at all, only by preserving the conditions in which individual creativity can flourish.

I commend the directors and staffs of the Soviet and American museums whose inspiration and hard work made possible this remarkable exchange of exhibits. I extend special thanks to Dr. Armand Hammer for coordinating this important event.

Ronald Reagan

Preface

In November 1985, President Ronald Reagan of the United States and General Secretary Mikhail Gorbachev of the Soviet Union held a summit meeting in Geneva, Switzerland. It was the first opportunity for the two leaders to meet face to face and share their views. World peace was the primary topic of the meeting and several methods were discussed between the two men of how a more stable world might be achieved. Each leader agreed that communication, cooperation, and exchanges would be essential ingredients to establishing mutual understanding between the people of their two nations, thus enhancing the chances for peace.

The summit concluded with, among other things, a cultural exchange agreement which has made it possible for me to arrange for this exhibition of forty great Impressionist and Post-Impressionist paintings from the Hermitage Museum in Leningrad and the Pushkin Museum of Fine Arts in Moscow. The works in this exhibition are not only the finest in Soviet collections but are also among the greatest masterpieces created by the artists represented.

In 1973, I arranged the first U.S. tour of important Impressionist and Post-Impressionist works from the Soviet Union. It was the first time that U.S. citizens were able to see in their own country such a major exhibition of masterpieces from the two leading museums of the U.S.S.R. In 1975 and 1979, I was able to organize two other exhibitions from Soviet collections including a U.S. tour in 1979 of the famous *Benois Madonna* by Leonardo da Vinci. In exchange for these exhibitions, masterpieces from my own collection and works from major U.S. museums have traveled to the Soviet Union for extended tours.

The current exhibition is also part of an exchange. In return for the forty works that are being shown at the National Gallery of Art, the Los Angeles County Museum of Art, and the Metropolitan Museum of Art, I have arranged for two exhibitions to tour the Soviet Union: 40 Impressionist and Post-Impressionist paintings from the National Gallery of Art, and 127 paintings and drawings from the Armand Hammer Collection. These exhibitions are touring the Soviet Union between February and December 1986.

It gives me great pleasure to be the first to arrange for exhibition exchanges under the new cultural agreement. These paintings travel to the people of both great nations as emissaries of peace and understanding, and they carry the promise of hope for a more peaceful world that was established by the spirit of Geneva.

Armand Hammer

Foreword

This exhibition—the first major cultural exchange to come after the Soviet-American Geneva summit in November 1985—presents in three of America's major cities forty of the great works of the Soviet Union's famed collections of Impressionist, Post-Impressionist, and early modern paintings. The cultural agreement signed by President Reagan and General Secretary Gorbachev has made possible the current exhibition. We would like particularly to thank the American industrialist and philanthropist, Dr. Armand Hammer, for his pivotal role in bringing this event about.

Art exhibitions tend to have long histories. This one is no exception. In June of 1983, an exhibition of Soviet-owned Impressionist and Post-Impressionist paintings opened at Baron Heinrich Thyssen-Bornemisza's villa in Lugano, Switzerland. Both the Director of the National Gallery of Art and Dr. Hammer made special visits to see the exhibition with the hope that it might be available for travel to the United States. The selection, clustered around major artists, seemed of exceptional quality. Without, however, a cultural agreement between the United States and the Soviet Union, further negotiations seemed fruitless at that time.

Dr. Hammer sent the *Codex Hammer* by Leonardo da Vinci to the U.S.S.R. in March of 1984 even before a cultural agreement had been reached. At that time Minister of Culture Pyotr Demichev assured Dr. Hammer that a loan of paintings similar to those shown in Lugano could be arranged for the United States—if a cultural agreement could be reached. Immediately after the Geneva accord was signed, the question was reopened with the Soviet authorities. Dr. Hammer personally pursued the idea in Moscow at the highest levels, and the outcome was an agreement whereby the exhibition would come to the National Gallery, the Los Angeles County Museum of Art, and The Metropolitan Museum of Art in New York. Through Dr. Hammer's good offices, the exhibition would be underwritten at all three sites by Occidental Petroleum Corporation.

The magnificent treasures housed in the Soviet museums have attained legendary status. Yet time, distance, and international boundaries prevent many Americans from experiencing the excitement and delight of seeing these astonishing collections at first hand. Now, two of the finest museums of the U.S.S.R.—the Hermitage Museum, Leningrad, and the Pushkin Museum of Fine Arts, Moscow—are sharing with us forty masterpieces by seven of the great Impressionist and early modern painters: Cézanne, Gauguin, Matisse, Monet, Renoir, van Gogh, and Picasso. These extraordinary works are a tribute to the advanced tastes of two great Moscow collectors, Ivan Morozov (1871–1921) and Sergei Shchukin (1854–1936), whose patronage of the arts during the early twentieth century excelled even that of the Stein and Cone families.

Morozov was a passionate collector of works by Monet, Pissarro, Renoir, van Gogh, and Cézanne, the recognized forerunner of twentieth-century painting. Shchukin, who began collecting in the 1890s, introduced the Impressionists to Russia with his 1897 purchase of paintings by Claude Monet. Like his compatriot Morozov, Shchukin soon preferred the tropical paintings of Gauguin and the controversial works of the Fauves and Cubists, gathering together 37 paintings by Matisse and 50 by Picasso. Both friends and rivals, these two Russian collectors recognized the significance of contemporary style and the birth of the modern era in French painting, building collections that were to become priceless trusts of two great Soviet museums.

We welcome this extraordinary exchange of magnificent paintings for its three-city tour and hope that the selections of Impressionist paintings from the National Gallery of Art, Washington, and from Dr. Armand Hammer's masterpiece paintings collection, both to be shown in Leningrad and Moscow, will serve to further the cultural bond between our two nations.

Our first thanks go to Dr. Hammer for making this exhibition possible. We are indebted also to Mr. Pyotr M. Demichev, Minister of Culture of the U.S.S.R., and the staffs of the Soviet museums, Professor Boris Piotrovsky, Director, and Mr. Vitali A. Suslov, Vice Director of the Hermitage, and Madame Irina Antonova, Director, and Madame Marina Bessonova of the Pushkin Museum. Appreciation is also extended to Mr. Dmitri Warygin, Deputy Director for International Relations, Mr. Valery Sorokin, Counselor for Bi-lateral and Cultural Affairs of the U.S.S.R., Madame Alla Butrova, Chief of the American and Western European Department, Ministry of Culture, and Mr. Albert Kostenevich, Curator of nineteenth and twentieth-century art at the Hermitage Museum.

We would also like to extend our thanks to Ambassador Arthur Hartman, the United States Ambassador to the U.S.S.R., and to Charles Wick, Director of the United States Information Agency. We are also grateful to the Federal Council on the Arts and the Humanities, and particularly Alice Whelihan, the Administrator of the Indemnity Program, for granting an Indemnity for the paintings lent to the Hermitage and Pushkin museums by the National Gallery in support and furtherance of this exhibition at all three American sites.

William McSweeny, President of Occidental International Corporation in Washington, Michael Bruk and Nina Vlassova, Occidental Petroleum Corporation in Moscow, and Dennis Gould, Patti Grammatikoulis, Quinton Hallett, and the staff of The Armand Hammer Foundation, have been particularly instrumental in the organization of the exhibition and to them we extend our deepest gratitude.

We would also like to thank the staffs of the participating museums. John Wilmerding, Deputy Director of the National Gallery, followed the evolution of the exhibition closely, and Charles Stuckey, Curator of Modern Painting at the Gallery, and David Bull, its Head of Painting Conservation, went to Moscow and Leningrad during the development of the lists and established very helpful contact with our colleagues in the Soviet museums. Shelley Fletcher and Ann Hoenigswald of the Gallery's conservation staff and C. Douglas Lewis of the curatorial staff were also helpful to the exhibition in the Soviet Union. The Gallery's Registrar, Mary Suzor, and Associate General Counsel, Elizabeth Croog, and its departments of Exhibitions and Loans and Modern Painting also deserve our special thanks. At the Los Angeles County Museum, Myrna Smoot, Assistant Director for Museum Programs, and Scott Schaefer, Curator of European Paintings and Sculpture, at the Metropolitan Museum of Art, James Pilgrim, Deputy Director, and Gary Tinterow, Assistant Curator of European Painting, were of great assistance. In addition to individuals at the participating museums, we extend special acknowledgment to John Rewald for his invaluable research assistance.

J. Carter Brown
Director
National Gallery of Art

Earl A. Powell III
Director
Los Angeles County Museum of Art

Philippe de Montebello
Director
The Metropolitan Museum of Art

Introduction

The art collections of two Soviet museums—the Hermitage in Leningrad and the Pushkin Museum of Fine Arts in Moscow—need no special introduction. They have always been major centers of attraction, both for Soviet art lovers and for visitors from abroad. The popularity of the Leningrad and Moscow collections is evidenced by a steady rise in numbers of visitors, as well as by a growing and diversified list of publications. Exhibitions of works sent abroad by the Hermitage and the Pushkin are also invariably greeted with enthusiastic response. Prior to World War II and up through the 1950s, such exhibitions were sporadic, and even then only individual canvases were, as a rule, sent abroad on loan. For the past twenty years, however, there has been a steady increase in the number of exhibitions, and their scope has widened considerably.

The Leningrad and Moscow museums have established and maintain firm ties with many eminent art centers and institutions in both hemispheres. Exhibitions are usually mounted on the basis of mutually beneficial exchanges. One would be hard-pressed to name a country which has not exhibited paintings from the Hermitage and the Pushkin. So far, the itinerary includes the USA, Canada, Venezuela, Cuba, Mexico, Australia, Poland, Czechoslovakia, Hungary, Yugoslavia, Sweden, Norway, Denmark, Holland, the Federal Republic of Germany, the German Democratic Republic, Switzerland, Austria, England, and Spain. France is our most active contact in Western Europe, with Italy in second place. Japan leads the way among non-European countries. Some very fruitful exchanges with American museums, particularly the Metropolitan Museum of Art, the National Gallery of Art, and the Los Angeles County Museum of Art, were arranged during the 1970s.

A number of Soviet exhibitions have been entirely based on collections of nineteenth- and twentieth-century art, by French artists for the most part. Modern French masterpieces were shown in Tokyo and Kyoto in 1966–1967. In 1972, a similar exhibition was mounted in Otterlo (the Netherlands), and another toured Washington, New York, Los Angeles, Fort Worth, Chicago, and Detroit the following year. A selection of works by Impressionist and Post-Impressionist painters was exhibited in Le Havre in 1973. A year later, a similar exhibition received a warm welcome in Japan and two years after that a nearly identical showing was mounted in Mexico. A fresh group of French works from the late nineteenth and early twentieth centuries went to Tokyo and Nara in 1984.

The 1983 exhibition in Lugano, Switzerland, was enthusiastically received. Slightly over half the canvases in that group, after their trip to Villa Favorita, the home and museum of Baron Hans Heinrich Thyssen-Bornemisza, were on the road again two years later, this time to Venice and

Rome. The Italian exhibition was rounded out by paintings which had not been sent to Switzerland but which were equally noteworthy as works of art.

The "Thyssen list," as the Lugano selection has been called, provided the basis for this exhibition, which will travel to Washington, Los Angeles, and New York. Individual modifications have, if anything, strengthened its appeal. Certain works already seen in the United States have been removed, to be replaced by works which rank as prime examples of the French artistic canon. Furthermore, some paintings from the Hermitage collection, such as Gauguin's *The Canoe (Te Vaa)* (cat. no. 22), Picasso's *Still Life with Skull* (cat. no. 36), and Matisse's *Conversation* (cat. no. 27), have never been exhibited abroad. While the American public is enjoying these masterpieces of modern French art from the Hermitage and the Pushkin museums, visitors to those two museums will be getting their first look at a comparable exhibition sent from the National Gallery of Art, Washington, D.C.

In both Soviet museums, which are famous for their collections of Western European paintings, the French holdings serve as a cornerstone. Two circumstances have combined to bring this about: the leading role played by French art in the eighteenth to early twentieth centuries, and the diverse cultural ties that were established between Russia and distant France in the mid-eighteenth century. One must remember the cultural and linguistic Francophilia of the Russian nobility and the Petersburg court in those days, the number of French painters who came to work in Russia, and the numerous purchases of French canvases made by Catherine the Great at the time she was founding the Hermitage (which set an example for the aristocracy to follow).

From the eighteenth century on, the propensities of Russian collectors were permanently linked to the art of France. B. N. Yusupov, a nobleman at Catherine's court, was a great connoisseur; his private collection was one of the best in Europe. N. A. Kushelev-Bezborodko was a man of completely different tastes. By his early death in 1862, he was the owner of a superb collection of European masterworks, whose tone was set by the French romantic and realist schools. After the Revolution of 1917, his gallery was acquired by the Hermitage.

Throughout the nineteenth century, the patricians who governed the affairs of artistic institutions and museums in the European states were remarkably slow in responding to new manifestations in art, so that individual collectors, who were willing to go out on a limb in defiance of reigning aesthetic dogmas, laid the foundations of future museums while at the same time supporting some pioneering artists. Actually, the Kushelev Gallery was opened to the public in the 1860s. Toward the end of the nineteenth century, the initiative passed from the aristocracy to the merchant class, whose more wealthy representatives embarked on the collection trail with the serious intention of benefiting Russian society. Members of rich Muscovite merchant families—the Tretyakovs, the Shchukins, the Morozovs—proved to be venturesome and intelligent collectors. The Tretyakov brothers set about creating the Tretyakov Gallery, which in time became an unparalleled treasure-house of Russian art. While the elder brother, Pavel Mikhailovich, was devoting his efforts to Russian painting, his younger sibling, Sergei Mikhailovich, was collecting "Frenchmen"—mostly painters from the Barbizon School and other realist masters. His collection is now in the Pushkin Museum.

The succeeding generation of collectors—S. I. Shchukin (1854–1936) and the brothers M. A. Morozov (1870–1903) and I. A. Morozov (1871–1921)—picked up where Sergei Tretyakov had left off. In 1897, Shchukin brought Monet's *Lilac in the Sun* from Paris. This was the first Impressionist painting Moscow had seen. Shchukin's Moscow town house was rapidly filled with paintings by Monet, Sisley, Cézanne, and Gauguin. He grew increasingly bold and far-sighted in his acquisitions, and seven years later, in 1904, he bought two works by Matisse, a painter whose name was not well known even among the avant-garde of Paris in those days. Shchukin had a compelling desire to make his collection the *dernier cri* in painting, as he understood the term. A true explorer, he had little interest in the latest fashion. Both he and I. A. Morozov deemed the masters of the new French school to be more than a mere curiosity, which is what many considered them to be. The two collectors realized that the Impressionists and those who followed after were a new and, moreover, highly important link in the chain of world culture. Matisse was later to recall that Shchukin's favorite pastime while in Paris was to visit the Louvre and study the Egyptian antiquities because he detected parallels between them and Cézanne's peasants. Shchukin and, later, Morozov unquestionably saw great social significance in their activities as collectors. The proof of this lies in the fact that each made a bequest of art to his hometown.

The Shchukin collection rapidly gained a reputation as one of Moscow's most outstanding cultural phenomena during the early years of this century. Even before the 1917 Revolution it was open to painters and the general public, thus providing a host of young Russian painters with a point of reference. I. A. Morozov's collection was still closed to the public at the time, but Shchukin's rival in the patronage of art maintained close contacts with the most talented Russian artists and acquired paintings not only by known painters such as Vrubel and Korovin, but also by the young Larionov and Chagall. The two collections played a prominent role in the establishment of fruitful ties between the art of Russia and its French counterpart.

Modern collectors and ordinary art lovers are usually amazed to hear that two men, ostensibly with no specialized training nor assistance from informed critics, and flying in the face of contemporary arbiters of taste and opinion, could amass such astonishing collections of masterworks. Of course, these men were extremely well versed and genuinely knowledgeable in all matters having to do with the latest artistic developments in France; but the main thing was that they both trusted their own instincts and feelings.

The extent of their activities is eloquently illustrated by the fact that they bought not only pictures of normal dimensions, which were relatively easy to transport back to Russia, but also huge decorative canvases intended for their town houses. And to paint those pieces they commissioned no lesser artists than Bonnard and Matisse. It is impressive just to scan the listing of eminent artists' names and note the numbers of pieces corresponding to each. Morozov, in actual fact, owned 6 Renoirs, 5 Sisleys, 11 Gauguins, 5 van Goghs, 13 Bonnards, and 10 Matisses. He was justifiably proud of his 18 Cézannes, each superlative in its own way. Shchukin possessed 8 Cézannes, but his total collection was larger. It included 13 Monets, 14 Gauguins, 7 Henri Rousseaus, 16 Derains, 37 Matisses, and 51 Picassos. The important point here is not the numbers, but the significance of the paintings themselves. So many of those works—Renoir's *Portrait of the Actress Jeanne Samary* (cat. no. 14), any of Cézanne's self-portraits, the decorative panels that Morozov commissioned from Bonnard, or *Dance* and *Music* which Matisse did for Shchukin—would be absolutely essential constituents in any history of the art of the period.

In his preferences and tastes, Shchukin was, by and large, the more radical of the two. He was also more decisive as a collector, relying primarily upon the evidence of his own eyes. The more cautious Morozov heeded the advice of artists and dealers with whom he was friendly. According to Matisse, Morozov would visit Ambroise Vollard, the art dealer, and ask to be shown the best Cézanne, while Shchukin, preferring to make his own selection, would have all the available Cézannes brought out. Shchukin did things on a more expansive scale; Morozov was more methodical. There was, for instance, an empty spot among Morozov's Cézannes, which was reserved for a landscape done late in the artist's life in Aix. He did not find what he was looking for until 1912, when he bought *Blue Landscape*, which became one of his favorite acquisitions.

The eminent Russian scholar of modern art, Abram Efros, put it this way:

> *Perhaps it should be described thus: the celebrity painters of Paris always presented themselves to Shchukin as though they were on a stage, in full make-up and tense; with Morozov they were more relaxed, more*

intimate, more "themselves." Just as a newcomer was beginning to be lionized in Paris, Shchukin would come swooping in, gather up everything he possibly could, and carry it off to Moscow, grinning gleefully whenever a neophyte rapidly became a maître *in Paris, while the things he had done turned out to be "at Shchukin's on Znamensk Lane."*

Morozov, on the other hand, would painstakingly seek out in a new artist something he alone saw, would finally make his choice, and, in doing so, would always add some perfect "corrective adjustment." "A Shchukin collection as amended by Morozov"—I would say this was the classical formula which defines our [Russian] collection of modern Western art.

Boris Ternovetz, the first director of the Museum of Modern Western Art, added:

I. A. Morozov collected with a passion scarcely to be expected in this outwardly phlegmatic, corpulent man. Once he arrived in Paris, Morozov wanted to do nothing but study the exhibitions and the stocks of the large art houses. Quite often, he was fortunate enough to get his hands on a Cézanne masterpiece which Vollard had been temporarily hiding in a "secret" cache, or to secure, by a quick decision, some pieces that had been earmarked for the best contemporary galleries. Morozov was altogether at home in the Paris art world, and he maintained a lively correspondence with artists and dealers, kept track of auctions, and sometimes took the risk of making a purchase without prior examination.
. . .

His collecting activities brought him into close contact with S. I. Shchukin, who had started his collection much earlier. While they were continually meeting in Paris, both collectors avoided any competition, preferring to view pieces together, in a friendly manner. While they shared a common purpose, their tastes manifestly differed. The more expansive Shchukin loved to "discover" an artist, to "launch" his career in the public eye. He found the element of risk enticing, and revelled in the amazed reactions of the numerous visitors to his town-house gallery. The circumspect and reserved Morozov strove less to keep abreast of the latest innovations, and was more eager to preserve a clear and complete conception of an era that had scarcely ended.

Both Moscow collectors, in addition to a doughty resolution, were prone to exhibit a certain mercantile patriarchalism. They adjudged their collecting activities to be a serious and respectable business. Moreover, in both cases, their hobby was something in which their entire families had to participate. Sergei Shchukin belonged to an amazing family, in which all four brothers were eminent collectors. Dmitri Shchukin had Moscow's best pre-revolutionary collection of Old Masters, which later became part of the holdings of the Museum of Fine Arts (now the Pushkin Museum of Fine Arts). Ivan Shchukin owned a number of Spanish paintings, but his real passion was rare books. Pyotr Shchukin, the eldest brother, primarily collected ancient Russian art treasures, which he later gave to the Historical Museum, but he also acquired several major Impressionist works, including Monet's *Woman in a Garden* (cat. no. 9). He ultimately gave them to his brother Sergei, who was head of the Shchukin business house.

Though Ivan Morozov started collecting later than Sergei Shchukin, the results he achieved were no less impressive. This millionaire factory owner had developed a genuine interest in art early in life. He and his elder brother Mikhail took lessons with Konstantin Korovin for two years. In the 1890s, some of Russia's best artists—painters such as Vrubel, Serov, and Korovin—would visit Mikhail in his town house. Ivan actually took his cue from Mikhail, who bought not only Russian paintings but French works as well. Of the pieces in this exhibition, Renoir's *Portrait of the Actress Jeanne Samary* and Gauguin's *The Canoe (Te Vaa)* originally belonged to Mikhail Morozov. An early death cut all this short, but from that point on, his younger brother considered it his duty to continue what they had begun together, and proceeded with redoubled energy.

The names of Sergei Shchukin and Ivan Morozov are indelibly inscribed in the history of the European artistic milieu of the early twentieth century. They both took a liking to modern art at a time when its following was still very small. The reward for their enthusiasm and unbiased attitudes was the enviable opportunity to choose from among the masterpieces of Renoir, Cézanne, Gauguin, van Gogh, Matisse, and Picasso. And the more perspicacious dealers—Durand-Ruel, Vollard, Kahnweiler—accommodated them, because they realized that their private collections were becoming what amounted to museums and "bridgeheads" from which the artistic avant-garde could advance to conquer new territory. The dealers were genuinely anxious to find a place for truly significant works of art in collections such as these.

Shortly after the October Revolution, in 1918, the Shchukin and Morozov collections were nationalized by a decree of the Council of People's Commissars and renamed the First and Second Museums of Modern European Painting. (The Second Museum opened its doors in 1919, somewhat later than the First.) Five years later, they were merged into the State Museum of Modern Western Art, which was the first museum of its kind in the world.

Some other collections were added to it: the Tretyakov Museum, for example, contributed the paintings that had been donated by Mikhail Morozov's widow. In 1928, the holdings of the Museum were brought together in one place—the former Morozov town house on Kropotkin Street (which now belongs to the U.S.S.R. Academy of Arts).

Later, as a result of government-level decisions on the redistribution of museum assets, many of the erstwhile Shchukin and Morozov canvases were transferred to the Hermitage. A far larger number, however—more than 450 Old Masters—were moved from Leningrad to Moscow and placed in the State Museum of Fine Art, which was named for Alexander Pushkin in 1937. (The Museum of Modern Western Art was made a branch of the Pushkin Museum.) When these exchanges were completed, paintings which only twenty or thirty years earlier had been the subject of bitter disputes and attacks could stand on an equal footing alongside classical masterpieces, first in the Hermitage and then in the Pushkin Museum (after the Museum of Modern Western Art was closed in 1948 and its collection definitively divided between the Hermitage and the Pushkin). Since the latter half of the 1950s, both museums have undergone a radical reorganization, which has installed the works of the Impressionists, Post-Impressionists, and the foremost painters of the early twentieth century in deservedly fitting places in two of the world's largest art museums.

A. G. Kostenevich
The Hermitage Museum
Leningrad

This exhibition contains works by Claude Monet, Renoir, Cézanne, Gauguin, van Gogh, Matisse, and Picasso, artists whose names brought distinction to the French school of painting at the turn of the century and whose creative achievements constituted a turning point in the development of twentieth-century art. Soviet collections include a number of paintings by major Impressionists dating from the period that represented the apogee of the Impressionist landscape genre—Renoir's *La Grenouillère* (cat. no. 12) and Monet's *Woman in a Garden* (cat. no. 9), to name two. They were produced by the young artists during the late 1860s and the 1870s, the time of the first Impressionist exhibitions. Both Renoir and Monet were later to embark upon long artistic odysseys marked by changes in their personal style and the genres in which they worked, but the work they did during the birth of Impressionism remains unsurpassed. Those early landscapes captivate us with the spontaneity of the impressions they convey and the energy of those rapid brushstrokes that commit the interplay of light and shade to canvas. There is an overwhelming sense of "joyful discovery" of the nooks and crannies of Paris and its environs.

Today, the joy one feels when looking at these sunlit canvases is mixed with a certain nostalgia. There was nothing random about Bellony's choice of title for the book she published shortly after the Impressionist centennial, *The Lost World of the Impressionists*. For people living today, at the end of the twentieth century, their paintings are very special indeed, offering us a candid and loving portrayal of a vanished world—the big sailboats on the Seine, the open-air dance floors in the heart of Paris, the vineyards just outside the city limits, and the almost bucolic mien of Montmartre.

The same atmosphere lives and breathes in the Impressionist portraits of the 1870s and early 1880s, best represented in our Renoirs. While these works perhaps lack a certain psychological depth, Renoir's remarkable *Lady in Black* (cat. no. 13) stands as an affirmation of the Impressionist approach to the portrait, for it captures the charming model's passing mood and fleeting facial expression. At the same time, Renoir continued to paint portraits tailored to the taste of the salons. There is an indication of this in his *Portrait of the Actress Jeanne Samary* (cat. no. 14), a work owned by the Hermitage. This type of representational art—a full-length human figure standing against a luxurious interior background—is in itself reminiscent of formal portraiture. However, the conscious self-assertion of models in official portraits is in contrast to Samary's vivacious facial expression and the artist's delightfully resonant palette.

Claude Monet is the best represented in Soviet collections, from his early composition *Le Déjeuner sur l'herbe* (Luncheon on the Grass) to his 1904 landscape, *Les Mouettes* (Seagulls). In the Hermitage's *Woman in a Garden*, which Monet himself considered to be a very significant work, he was primarily concerned with the artistic effects of sunlight, a problem he was to work on with Renoir in Argenteuil and Bougival during 1869. The result of these joint efforts was the series *La Grenouillère*, scenes from the little *al fresco* café of that name near Chatou. This islet in the Seine was one of the Parisians' favorite spots for bathing and sailing. Renoir's *Oarsmen at Chatou* is in Washington's National Gallery of Art. The Pushkin Museum of Fine Arts has loaned Renoir's marvelous *La Grenouillère*, 1869 (cat. no. 12), the brilliant début of Renoir the Impressionist, to this exhibition.

In Monet's mature works, which are a vivid embodiment of Impressionism, there is a definite tendency to nullify the sense of depth by letting the brushstrokes run together and by maintaining the same intensity of color across the entire surface of the canvas. The artist is clearly working for a two-dimensional effect in his painting. In a logical development of his work on techniques of this kind, Monet was ultimately drawn to the art of muralism. He thus came to grips with the problem of bringing easel painting out of its isolation, of synthesizing it with other forms of art. He submitted several large panels, designed to be used as interior décor, to the Third Impressionist Exhibition. Two of them, *Corner of the Garden at Montgeron* and *The Pond at Montgeron* (cat. nos. 10 and 11), are in this exhibition.

No survey of the art of the late nineteenth century would be complete without mention of the works of Cézanne, van Gogh, and Gauguin in Soviet museums. The years 1872–1879 have come to be known as Cézanne's Impressionist period. In 1872 he and Pissarro went to Pontoise to paint in the open air. His palette became appreciably lighter; it vibrated with rich green and golden hues, and the darker tones vanished altogether. Cézanne abandoned the technique of contouring, and began instead to use color as his compositional medium. This brought a greater plasticity and gravity to his forms. The still life *Vase of Flowers* (cat. no. 3), in the Hermitage, is a typical experiment along these lines. It is evidence of a search for new color combinations and an attempt to employ spots of color in the structuring of compositions. But in this still life, as in the Cézanne landscape *The Property of "Les Mathurins" in the Hermitage Quarter of Pontoise* (cat. no. 2), in the Pushkin Museum, we see none of the color reflections or the sunlight effects to which the Impressionists were so partial. In both the landscape and the still life, Cézanne was interested in forms that are identified by color but not dissolved in it.

After 1879, Cézanne became deeply involved in the constructional problems of solid plasticity in three-dimensional objects and integrated spherical space. His favorite subjects were the landscape and the still life, where every motif was apt to embody the idea of the unity of the universe in an eternal state of becoming. He was at his creative peak. The *Still Life with Milk Can, Carafe, and Coffee Bowl* (cat. no. 4), in the Hermitage, gives some idea of this experimental genre which was so extremely important to Cézanne. Art experts have frequently stressed that, merely by electing to paint still lifes, Cézanne distanced himself considerably from the Impressionists. Cézanne's still lifes demonstrate the eternity of matter, the unity of its diverse elements, the similarity of those elements, and the possibility of mutual metamorphosis. The objects in *Still Life with Milk Can, Carafe, and Coffee Bowl* stand in a complex relationship with the space which Cézanne has created. The fruit seems to be "rolling off" the tabletop, instead of just lying on it; the tablecloth is rucked up into a miniature mountain and "hangs" in space turned toward the viewer.

Cézanne's later works, in addition to creating an impression of spatial depth, also structure space on the vertical by use of color. The composition thus exerts an intense impact on the viewer, who is compelled to spend time examining the landscape. The element of time thus becomes part of the painter's stock-in-trade. These compositional techniques allowed Cézanne to create a truly cosmic image of the universe in the Mont Sainte-Victoire landscape series. In the Soviet collections it is possible to trace all the steps which Cézanne took in meeting this challenge, from *La Montagne Sainte-Victoire*, one of the earliest scenic paintings, to the magnificent *Mont Sainte-Victoire Seen from Les Lauves* (cat. no. 8), which was completed shortly before the painter's death.

The Moscow and Leningrad museums also contain some of Cézanne's noteworthy portrayals of people. He considered the human being to be an integral part of the universe. The tension and imbalance of his justly acclaimed *Mardi Gras* (Pushkin Museum) make this painting a foretaste of Expressionism and Cubism. These tendencies are most evident in *Woman in Blue* (cat. no. 7), in the Hermitage. It is very clear how much Russian artists of the Jack of Diamonds ("Bubnovy valet") group learned from this. But Cézanne's concept of man's role in the universe, his ability to immortalize his contemporaries in a manner reminiscent of the Renaissance masters, is best seen in his Smokers series. *The Smoker* (Hermitage) depicts a peasant who is, in L. Venturi's words, "as individual as a portrait, as universal as an idea, as imposing as a monument, as strong as a clear conscience."

Some of the works of Vincent van Gogh found in Soviet museums, the earliest of which were painted when he first arrived in Arles and the last at the very end of his life in Auvers, are among the indisputable masterpieces of this great artist. The *Portrait of Doctor Félix Rey* (cat. no. 25) is rendered in the expressionist style typical of van Gogh, with the main accents on the subject's facial expression and a dynamic background scored with tentacle-like curlicues and blood-red droplets of paint. Van Gogh's confinement in the asylum at Saint-Rémy is represented by *The Prison Courtyard* (cat. no. 26), a consummate work of art which symbolizes utter human despair.

Most of the Gauguin paintings from the extensive collections of I. A. Morozov and, more particularly, S. I. Shchukin, were done during the artist's first two visits to Tahiti. In *Are You Jealous? (Aha oe feii?)* (cat. no. 19), a portrayal of native women beside a pool, earth and water are depicted in a schematic manner and reduced to dense, contiguous patches of color on a single screen-like surface. Gauguin understood the plane surface as a substance which is capable of infinite reformulation, as an active force field, in which the structures of all possible objects are embedded and to which all those objects may return, becoming a plane once again. Gauguin made this discovery at Pont-Aven, and by the time of his first visit to Tahiti he was making a conscious effort to restrain himself from an overly documentary approach and redundant detail. He was impelled to understand and conceptualize the exoticism of his alien surroundings, to make it his own, to order it in his own mind. Gauguin's synthetism found renewed life in Tahiti. It was the means whereby he contrived to control the elemental interplay of natural forces, the luxuriant excess of the exotic milieu shown in *Tahitian Pastoral Scene* (cat. no. 20), which is so alluring to the European, so "fragrant" (*Noa Noa*) but at the same time so poisonous, overwhelming, and so capable of consuming human individuality. On the other hand, the techniques that Gauguin used in his synthetizing style underline the strangeness of the countryside he was painting, the enormous gulf separating it from the shapes and the color combinations familiar to the European eye. Those techniques transformed the Tahitian setting into the symbol of a different reality created by the human imagination, into *Reveries (Nave Nave Moe)* (cat. no. 21) in the Hermitage; in other words, they made Oceania more exotic than it really was.

It is the conceptual density of Gauguin's paintings more than anything else which ties them to the art of the nineteenth century, and, in particular, to European symbolism. But, for all the similarity of theme and subject matter, Gauguin and the European symbolists were speaking essentially different languages. Gauguin rejected the refined guile of civilized European discourse in favor of the surpassingly graphic idiom of primitive peoples, because of its forthrightness, its full-blooded imagery. It would be rash to criticize Gauguin for giving an overly serious reading to eternal themes. *Her Name is Vaïraumati (Vaïraumati tei oa)* (cat. no. 17), in the Pushkin Museum, offers two renditions of a scene from the Maori myth of the encounter between the god Horo and the lovely Vaïraumati. The real Horo and Vaïraumati are seen in a Polynesian wood-carving set in the background of the painting, but the title actually refers to the Tahitian woman who is portrayed seated on a brightly colored carpet. This personification of Vaïraumati, the Earth Mother, is also a cigarette-smoking *vahine* of questionable virtue.

On analysis, it proves impossible to categorize Gauguin's paintings as ornamentalism triumphant, as an unbridled, elemental adherence to form, because beneath that form there lies a figurative-conceptual substratum which has its own *histoire* and its own subject matter. But one cannot approach this aspect too seriously either, since alongside that substratum and coexisting easily with it there is a playfulness, a sense of irony and *sang-froid* emanating from the artist himself. It is the interaction of these three levels which attunes Gauguin's art to the twentieth century.

The creative beginnings of two preeminent artists of the twentieth century, Matisse and Picasso, are represented in Soviet museums by some world-famous works. The exhibition includes Matisse's masterpieces from his mature Fauvist period—the *Goldfish* (cat. no. 29) and *Nasturtiums with "La Danse"* (cat. no. 31), panels from the Pushkin Museum, and the renowned *Conversation* (cat. no. 27) from the Hermitage.

The Picasso paintings selected for this retrospective are masterpieces. The American public will have the opportunity to see this artist's remarkable *Harlequin and His Companion* and *Portrait of the Tailor José Maria Soler* (cat. nos. 33 and 34). The study *Woman from Mallorca* (cat. no. 35) will be of particular interest to experts and to art lovers, since it was painted while Picasso was working on *The Family of Saltimbanques*, a renowned work from his Pink Period, which is in the National Gallery of Art in Washington. The early and mature Cubist periods are illustrated in this exhibition by the splendid *Three Women* and *Portrait of Ambroise Vollard* (cat. nos. 39 and 40), unquestionably two of the finest portraits produced in the twentieth century.

M. Bessonova
Pushkin Museum of Fine Arts
Moscow

List of Plates

1. Paul Cézanne, *Self-Portrait with Cap*, The Hermitage Museum
2. Paul Cézanne, *The Property of "Les Mathurins" in the Hermitage Quarter of Pontoise*, The Pushkin Museum
3. Paul Cézanne, *Vase of Flowers*, The Hermitage Museum
4. Paul Cézanne, *Still Life with Milk Can, Carafe, and Coffee Bowl*, The Hermitage Museum
5. Paul Cézanne, *Large Pine Tree near Aix*, The Hermitage Museum
6. Paul Cézanne, *Pool with Bridge*, The Pushkin Museum
7. Paul Cézanne, *Woman in Blue*, The Hermitage Museum
8. Paul Cézanne, *Mont Sainte-Victoire Seen from Les Lauves*, The Pushkin Museum
9. Claude Monet, *Woman in a Garden*, The Hermitage Museum
10. Claude Monet, *Corner of the Garden at Montgeron*, The Hermitage Museum
11. Claude Monet, *Pond at Montgeron*, The Hermitage Museum
12. Pierre Auguste Renoir, *Bathing in the Seine (La Grenouillère)*, The Pushkin Museum
13. Pierre Auguste Renoir, *Lady in Black*, The Hermitage Museum
14. Pierre Auguste Renoir, *Portrait of the Actress Jeanne Samary*, The Hermitage Museum
15. Paul Gauguin, *Self-Portrait*, The Pushkin Museum
16. Paul Gauguin, *The Flowers of France (Te Tiare Farani)*, The Pushkin Museum
17. Paul Gauguin, *Her Name is Vaïraumati (Vaïraumati Tei Oa)*, The Pushkin Museum
18. Paul Gauguin, *The Dead Tree (Matamoe)*, The Pushkin Museum
19. Paul Gauguin, *Are You Jealous? (Aha Oe Feii)*, The Pushkin Museum
20. Paul Gauguin, *Tahitian Pastoral Scene*, The Hermitage Museum
21. Paul Gauguin, *Reveries (Nave Nave Moe)*, The Hermitage Museum
22. Paul Gauguin, *The Canoe (Te Vaa)*, The Hermitage Museum

23. Paul Gauguin, *Relax (Eiaha Ohipa)*, The Pushkin Museum

24. Vincent van Gogh, *A View of the Arena in Arles*, The Hermitage Museum

25. Vincent van Gogh, *Portrait of Doctor Félix Rey*, The Pushkin Museum

26. Vincent van Gogh, *The Prison Courtyard*, The Pushkin Museum

27. Henri Matisse, *Conversation*, The Hermitage Museum

28. Henri Matisse, *Spanish Woman with a Tambourine*, The Pushkin Museum

29. Henri Matisse, *Goldfish*, The Pushkin Museum

30. Henri Matisse, *Moroccan in Green*, The Hermitage Museum

31. Henri Matisse, *Nasturtiums with "La Danse,"* The Pushkin Museum

32. Henri Matisse, *Bouquet on the Veranda*, The Hermitage Museum

33. Pablo Picasso, *Harlequin and His Companion*, The Pushkin Museum

34. Pablo Picasso, *Portrait of the Tailor José Maria Soler*, The Hermitage Museum

35. Pablo Picasso, *Woman from Mallorca*, The Pushkin Museum

36. Pablo Picasso, *Still Life with Skull*, The Hermitage Museum

37. Pablo Picasso, *House and Trees*, The Pushkin Museum

38. Pablo Picasso, *Seated Woman Holding a Fan*, The Hermitage Museum

39. Pablo Picasso, *Three Women*, The Hermitage Museum

40. Pablo Picasso, *Portrait of Ambroise Vollard*, The Pushkin Museum

Catalogue

Paul Cézanne

(Aix-en-Provence 1839–
Aix-en-Provence 1906)

Cézanne was born in 1839, the son of a rich Provençal banker. Against his father's wishes, he left law school and enrolled at the Académie Suisse (1861), where he met Pissarro and other future Impressionists. During the Franco-Prussian War, Cézanne avoided conscription by taking refuge at L'Estaque, outside Marseilles, where he first worked after nature. After the war, he returned to Paris and resumed contact with Pissarro, whom he came to regard as his master. Cézanne's association with Pissarro is crucial. As they worked together—often on the same motif—Cézanne's palette lightened; he perceived how to analyze color and tone, and arrived at new ways of relating these two elements. Unlike the other Impressionists, he was not interested in using color to catch fleeting effects of light but to build up form and structure, even a measure of perspective.

In 1886, Cézanne's father died, leaving a substantial fortune. The artist could now retire to the family's handsome house on the outskirts of Aix, the Jas de Bouffan, and devote himself to painting how and what he liked: the arid beauty of the Provençal scene—above all the Mont Sainte-Victoire that rears up northeast of the town—and portraits of his wife and other models patient enough to put up with hundreds of sittings.

"When color has its greatest richness, then form has its plenitude." Here in a nutshell is what Cézanne's later work is about. But it is to the artist's credit that he never turned this dictum into a picture-making formula. On the contrary, his approach was always intuitive, never theoretical.

The Master of Aix, as he came to be known, never won the official recognition that he craved. Nevertheless, he participated in Impressionist exhibitions in 1874 and 1877 and the Salon of 1882. In 1895, his first solo exhibition took place at the Vollard Gallery. Before he died, he had the satisfaction of being hailed as the undisputed master of a new generation of painters: Maurice Denis, Emile Bernard, Bonnard, and Vuillard. By the year of his death—Cézanne had vowed that he would "die painting," and he did—Matisse and the Fauves were already modifying their ideas in the light of Cézanne's discoveries; and the future Cubists were about to push the artist's concepts to their logical end in their quest for a new pictorial language.

Paul Cézanne
1839–1906

1. *Self-Portrait With Cap,*
c. 1873

Oil on canvas, 53 × 38 cm

Hermitage Museum, inv. no. 6512

Provenance: H. Havemeyer collection, New York; 1909, I. Morozov collection (bought for 12,000 francs in Durand-Ruel's gallery, where it was sent by Mary Cassatt); 1918, Second Museum of Modern Western Painting, Moscow; 1923, Museum of Modern Western Art, Moscow; since 1930, Hermitage, Leningrad.

Lionello Venturi was the first to assign this canvas to the 1873–1875 period, a time in which the painter had close contact with Pissarro. The painting may be described as belonging to Cézanne's Impressionist period. Its simplicity and austerity remind us of the *Self-Portrait* by Pissarro (1873) in the Louvre. Although Pissarro painted his *Portrait of Cézanne* in 1874, it would not be correct to date the Hermitage *Self-Portrait* on the basis of the similarities of the main figures because Cézanne's appearance remained approximately the same for many years. John Rewald assigns the picture to c. 1875.

Douglas Cooper has suggested earlier dates, 1872–1873, and states that *Self-Portrait* was painted before Cézanne worked with Pissarro. Cooper offers as proof of his conclusion that the entire painting was executed with a painter's knife. This would mean that *Self-Portrait* was painted by Cézanne in Pontoise, or more probably in Auvers, where the painter moved in early 1873.

The portrait is an outstanding example of Cézanne's skill. It occupies a prominent place among the works of Cézanne's earlier period, as it preserves the expressiveness of the artist's work so evident during the years of the previous so-called Romantic period.

Paul Cézanne
1839–1906

2. *The Property of "Les Mathurins" in the Hermitage Quarter of Pontoise,* 1875–1877

Oil on canvas, 58 × 71 cm

Pushkin Museum, inv. no. 3410

Provenance: 1907, G. Viau collection, Paris, no. 12; 1909, E. Druet collection, Paris; 1909, I. Morozov collection, Moscow; 1918, First Museum of Modern Western Painting, Moscow; 1923, Museum of Modern Western Art, Moscow; since 1948, Pushkin Museum, Moscow.

Cézanne often painted at Auvers and at nearby Pontoise until 1877. To some degree, his increasing preoccupation with landscape was because of the influence of Pissarro and the other Impressionists. Working together, Pissarro and Cézanne frequently painted one and the same motif. It is quite possible that Cézanne conceived the present canvas on Pissarro's advice (in any case, such is the opinion of Bernard Dorival). Also at Pontoise, Cézanne painted some views of the Quartier de l'Ermitage, which is close in motif to the Pushkin Museum picture (Venturi, nos. 170 and 176). The most probable dating of this picture (also known as *Paysage de Gisora, Le Clos des Mathurins, Route de l'Ermitage à Pontoise*) is 1875–1877, although this date has not met with general acceptance.

Paul Cézanne
1839–1906

3. *Vase of Flowers*, 1874–1875

Oil on canvas, 55 × 46 cm

Signed, bottom left: Cézanne

Hermitage Museum, inv. no. 8954

Provenance: V. Chocquet collection, Paris; (his widow's auction, July 1–4, 1899, no. 29) Durand-Ruel Gallery; 1904, Shchukin collection, Moscow; 1918, First Museum of Modern Western Painting, Moscow; 1923, Museum of Modern Western Art, Moscow; since 1948, Hermitage, Leningrad.

Venturi ascribed this painting to the group of still life paintings (nos. 179–184) that he suggested were executed between 1873 and 1875. Many of the paintings of this group would therefore have been created in Auvers, where Cézanne lived in 1873–1874 with Dr. Gachet and often met with Pissarro. Venturi does not exclude the possibility that the still life paintings were done in Auvers, even though Cézanne spent part of 1874 and 1875 in Paris and Aix. Douglas Cooper has suggested that the dates of these paintings should be adjusted to 1874–1875. John Rewald suggests a later date, c. 1877.

The artist's approach to the subject differs in each of these paintings in composition and in method of applying paint. Of this group, *Flowers in a Vase* (Venturi, no. 181, Paris, private collection) is the most similar to the Hermitage work, as it depicts the same vase. Of all the works of the middle 1870s, these two still life paintings stand out as the most finished.

This picture is signed by Cézanne, which is rare in his work. The signature on this and the other still lifes of the group may indicate that Cézanne wanted to sell his work.

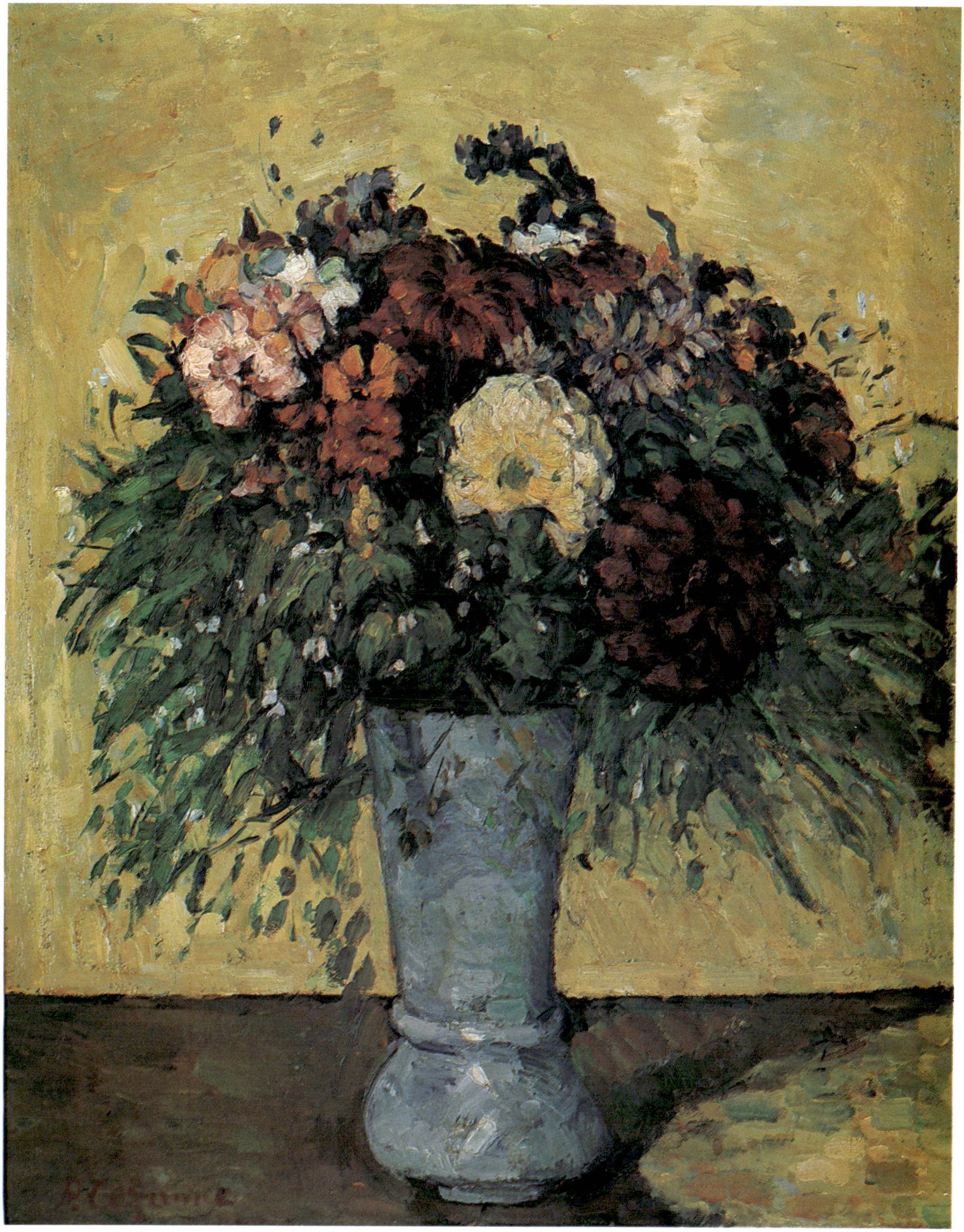

Paul Cézanne
1839–1906

4. *Still Life With Milk Can, Carafe, and Coffee Bowl,* c. 1879–1880

Oil on canvas, 45 × 55 cm

Hermitage Museum, inv. no. 9026

Provenance: H. Havemeyer collection, New York; 1894, Durand-Ruel Gallery, New York; 1895, Durand-Ruel Gallery, Paris; 1903, Shchukin collection, Moscow; 1918, First Museum of Modern Western Painting, Moscow; 1923, Museum of Modern Western Art, Moscow; since 1948, Hermitage, Leningrad.

Venturi assigns this canvas to a group of paintings dated 1879–1882 that have as their subject various objects depicted before a background of leaf-patterned wallpaper. In his view, the wallpaper might have been found either in Cézanne's home at Melun, where he lived in 1879 and 1880, or at Rue de l'Ouest, where the painter lived in 1881 and 1882. Later researchers have tried to correct the practice of assembling the paintings into groups, concluding that the wallpaper with geometric or leaf patterns shown in Cézanne's works of the time could have been in many places, even in Aix. It has been the tendency of Sterling, Gowing, Rivière, and others to narrow the time period in which the still life pictures, which include the wallpaper motif, were painted. The present canvas was most probably painted around 1879–1880.

Cézanne located the same objects in various ways in front of various types of wallpaper. A metal milk jug, decanter, painted bowl, and fruit are also shown in other compositions (see Venturi, nos. 338 and 340). No. 338 is most directly related to the Hermitage painting, as it also has a crumpled napkin in the center of the composition and a milk jug at the left, with leaf-patterned wallpaper in the background.

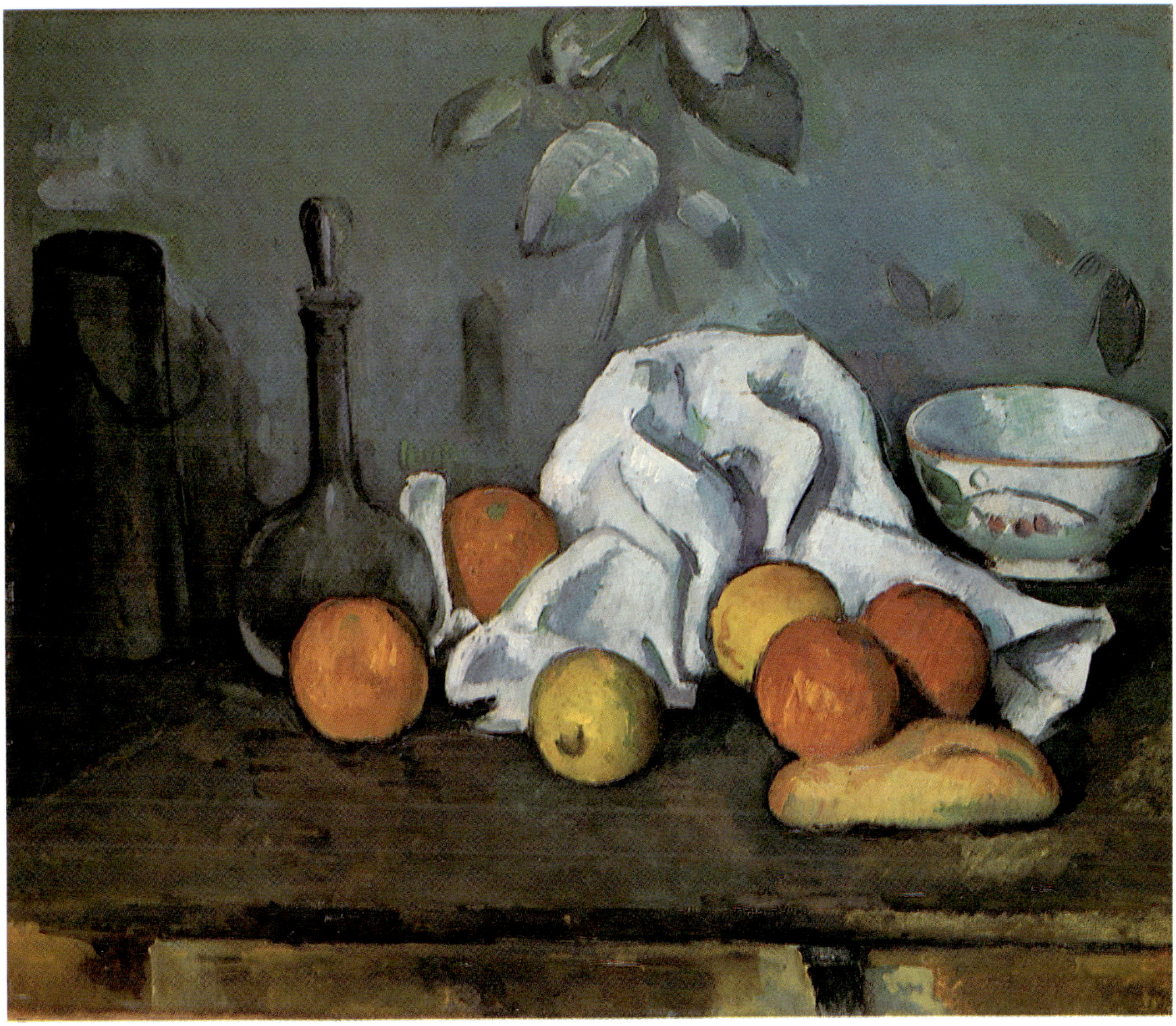

Paul Cézanne
1839–1906

5. *Large Pine Tree Near Aix,*
   c. 1895–1897

Oil on canvas, 72 × 91 cm

Hermitage Museum, inv. no. 8963

Provenance: Vollard Gallery, Paris; 1908, I. Morozov collection (acquired from Vollard for 15,000 francs); 1918, Second Museum of Modern Western Painting, Moscow; 1923, Museum of Modern Western Art, Moscow; since 1948, Hermitage, Leningrad.

It is quite possible that some special personal reasons prompted Cézanne to paint the same pine tree shown in this painting several times. The area represented in these paintings is in the Arc River Valley near Aix. In 1885–1887, Cézanne painted *Great Pine in Montbriant* (former collection of Lecomte, Venturi, no. 459); the watercolor, *Great Pine* (Venturi, no. 1024), probably belongs to the same time period. There is no doubt that the painter showed the same tree in all of these works. Although Venturi dated the Hermitage canvas to the same time as *Great Pine in Montbriant*, those who assign it to a later period may be more accurate. For example, Cooper suggests the dates 1889–1891 on the basis of his analysis of the colors used in the work. John Rewald suggests the dates 1890–1895. Nina Yavorskaya suggested a later date of 1895–1897, and Theodore Reff agreed with her. It is well known that around 1897 Cézanne often worked in Montbriant at his brother-in-law's estate. The Hermitage painting differs from *The Great Pine in Montbriant* in approach to its subject and better composition. The tree trunk is thicker in this painting, and the surrounding small trees at its base are taller.

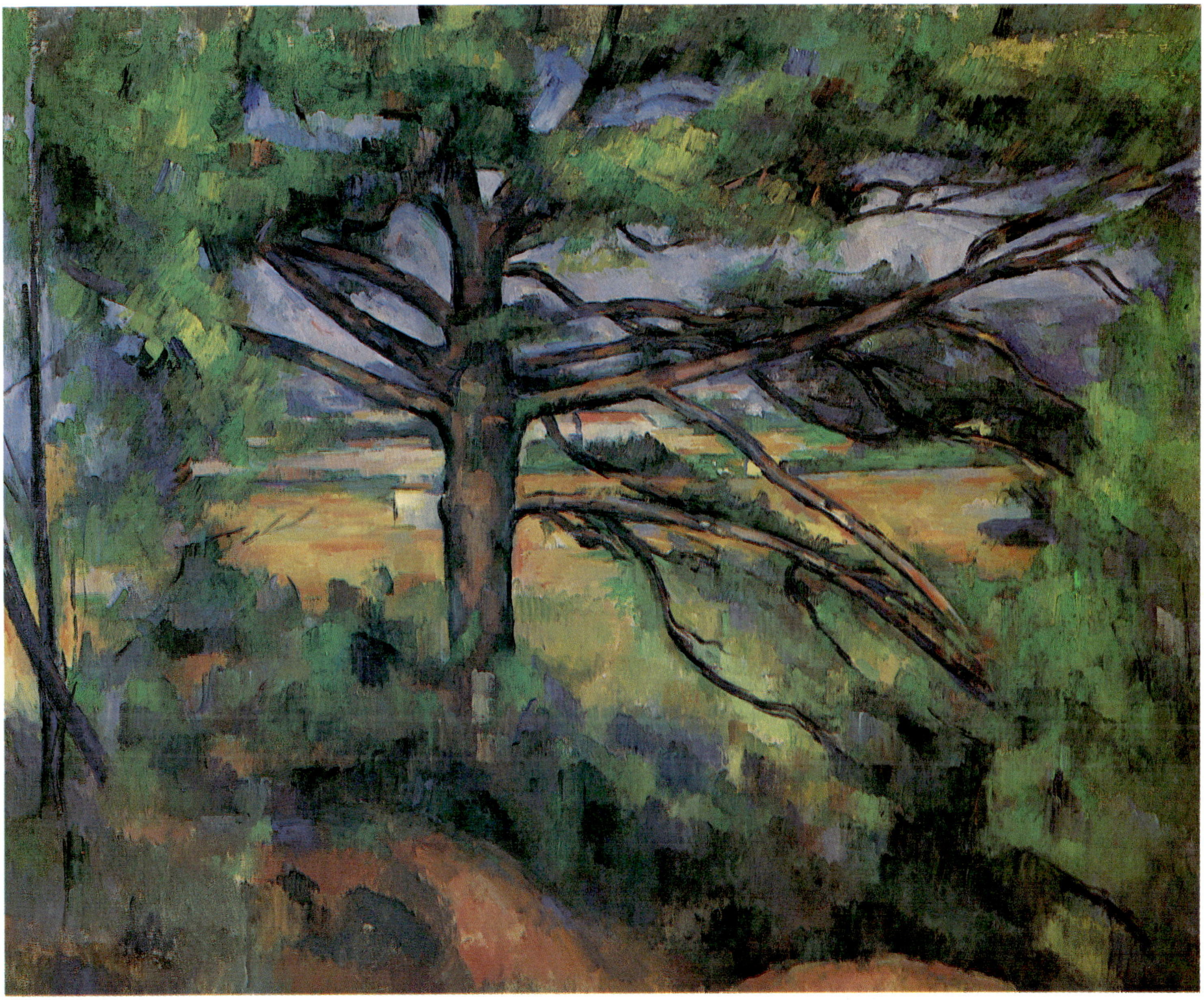

Paul Cézanne
1839–1906

6. *Pool With Bridge,* c. 1895–1898

Oil on canvas, 64 × 79 cm

Pushkin Museum, inv. no. 3417

Provenance: 1911, Vollard collection, Paris; 1911, I. Morozov collection; 1918, Second Museum of Modern Western Painting, Moscow; 1923, Museum of Modern Western Art, Moscow; since 1948, Pushkin Museum, Moscow.

Most scholars who have studied Cézanne's work date this painting to 1888–1890. It shows some stylistic connection with *The Banks of the Marne* in the Hermitage collection. The landscape is executed in thin liquid paint and exhibits the orderly brushwork and similarly shaped strokes that are applied at an angle to one another. This picture clearly demonstrates those principles used by Cubist painters several years later.

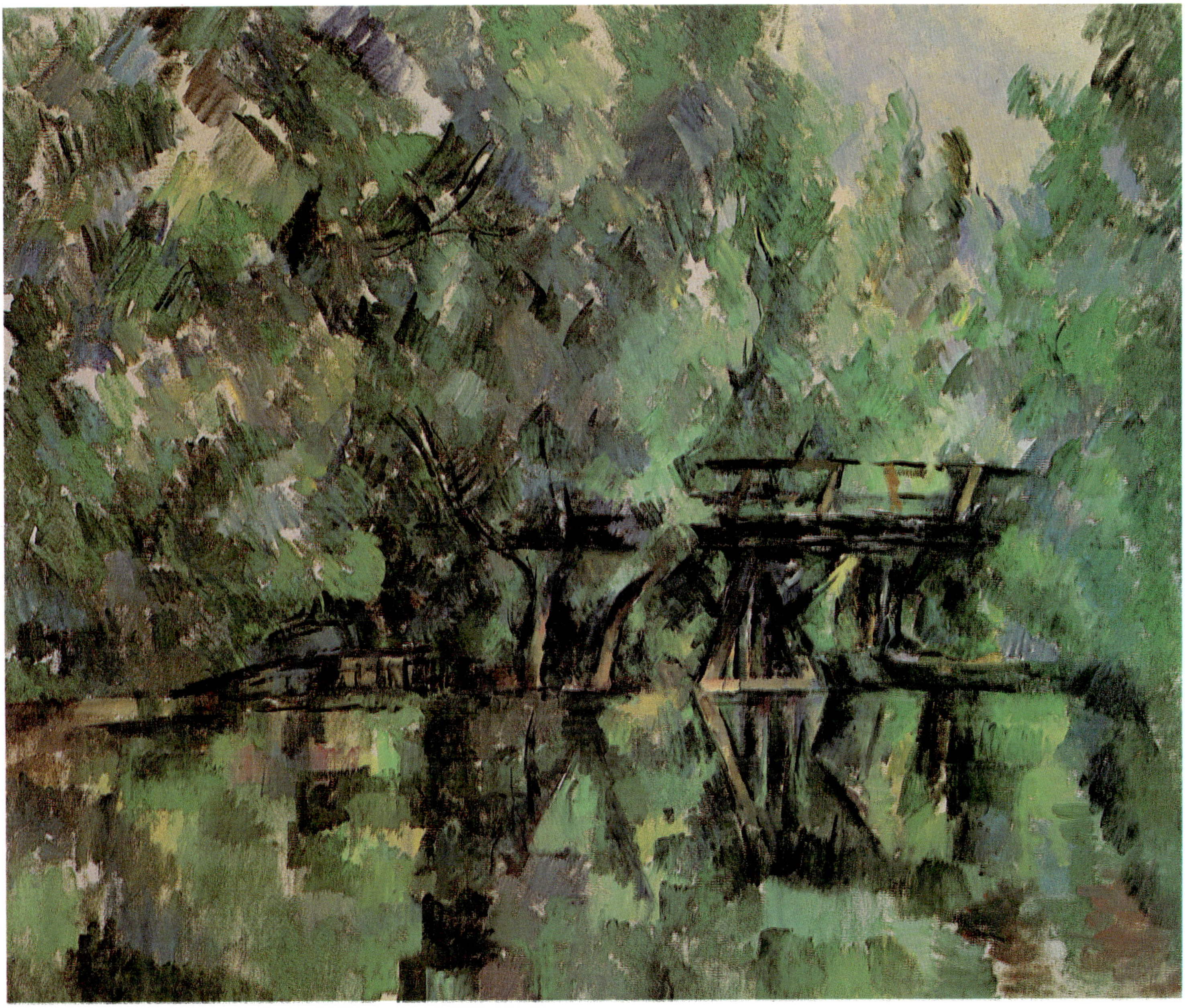

Paul Cézanne
1839–1906

7. *Woman in Blue*,
c. 1900

Oil on canvas, 90 × 73.5 cm

Hermitage Museum, inv. no. 8990

Provenance: Shchukin collection, Moscow; 1913, First Museum of Modern Western Painting, Moscow; 1923, Museum of Modern Western Art, Moscow; since 1948, Hermitage, Leningrad.

Cézanne experts differ considerably in determining the date of this painting. Rewald assigns it to c. 1904. On the basis of iconographic and stylistic similarities, Venturi referred *Woman in Blue* to a group of works dated by him to the 1900–1904 period. This group includes *An Italian Woman Bent over the Table* (Rosenthal collection, New York), *An Old Woman with Rosaries* (National Gallery, London), *Lady with a Book* (Phillips Collection, Washington, D.C.), and *Portrait of Madame Cézanne* (Barnes Foundation, Merion, Pennsylvania). However, the dates assigned to individual works in this group of paintings are not considered quite as monolithic now, and each receives a different date in the literature.

The Hermitage painting is usually compared to the *Lady with a Book*, in which the model wears the same dress and hat. In the catalogue of the exhibition of Cézanne's late works (Museum of Modern Art, New York, 1977), Rewald mistakenly suggested that the same woman posed for both paintings. In the Rewald catalogue for this exhibition, *Woman in Blue* (no. 54) is referred to the 1902–1906 period. On the other hand, Lawrence Gowing, one of the organizers of the same exhibition, offered the earlier 1892–1896 time period, leaving the 1902–1903 period to *Lady with a Book*. The problem of assigning dates to these paintings is further complicated by the fact that Cézanne used the same subjects many times over a period of several years. Gowing believes that *Woman in Blue* was painted in Aix in a studio at Rue Boulegon, and Rewald suggests that the narrow interior of the composition also refers to the Rue Boulegon. However, these arguments are not sufficient in themselves to convince scholars that the painting was done in Aix and not in Paris.

Another detail of the *Woman in Blue*—the rug in the lower right—is also depicted in *Italian Woman Bent over the Table* and in the still life *Apples and Oranges* (D'Orsay Museum, Paris, Venturi, no. 732), now usually dated 1895–1900.

At the exhibition of Cézanne's later works, the "Italian" was dated about 1900, and it can be argued that *An Old Woman with Rosaries* also belongs to the same period. These two canvases are closer in concept and execution to *Woman in Blue* than are any of the paintings in the group mentioned by Venturi, which allows one to conclude that the Hermitage painting was indeed made around 1900.

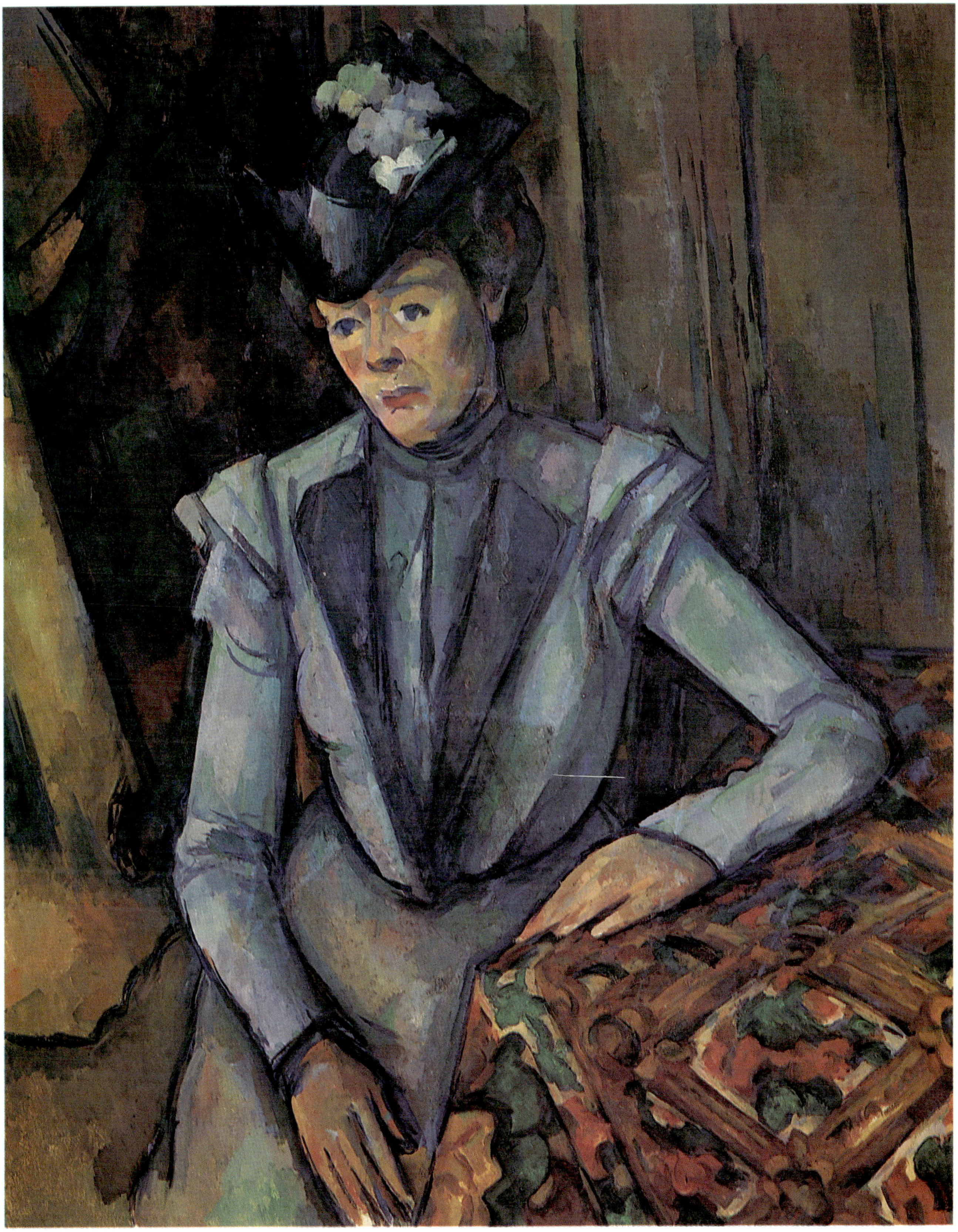

Paul Cézanne
1839–1906

8. *Mont Sainte-Victoire Seen from Les Lauves*, 1904–1906

Oil on canvas, 80 × 73 cm

Pushkin Museum, inv. no. 3339

Provenance: A. Vollard Gallery, Paris; 1911, Shchukin collection, Moscow; 1918, First Museum of Modern Western Paintings, Moscow; 1923, Museum of Modern Western Art, Moscow; since 1948, Pushkin Museum, Moscow.

Cézanne painted and drew Mont Sainte-Victoire about fifty times. On the basis of this canvas' specific features, Gowing dated the Pushkin Museum painting 1906 (in spite of some facts, he considered it the latest Cézanne painting of the Sainte-Victoire mountain). The Pushkin Museum landscape is executed in bright, radiant colors with almost square brush strokes. The impulsiveness and dynamism of the canvas produce a deep impression on the spectator. Masson writes in reference to this painting that during the last period of Cézanne's work, "la concentration est telle qu'elle explose. Elle est 'un phénomène futur' " (A. Masson, *Le Tombeau de Cézanne*, Paris, 1956, p. 38).

However, this painting is present in Cézanne's portrait painted by M. Denis in 1905 at Aix, and it is why Venturi dated the landscape 1905. In addition, on the back of the canvas' stretcher there was formerly a label with the words: "Exposition—1905," which made some experts think that the painting was exhibited in the Autumn Salon that opened on October 18, 1905, and included ten Cézanne canvases under the general title of "Paysages de Provence." The latter proof was questioned by Rewald in his 1978 catalogue of Cézanne's work, as Rewald thought that the label could have belonged to an exhibition in Vollard's gallery (Vollard had owned the canvas). Therefore, A. Barskaya, E. Georgievskaya, and Venturi date the Pushkin Museum painting to 1905, while Gowing and Rewald date it to 1906.

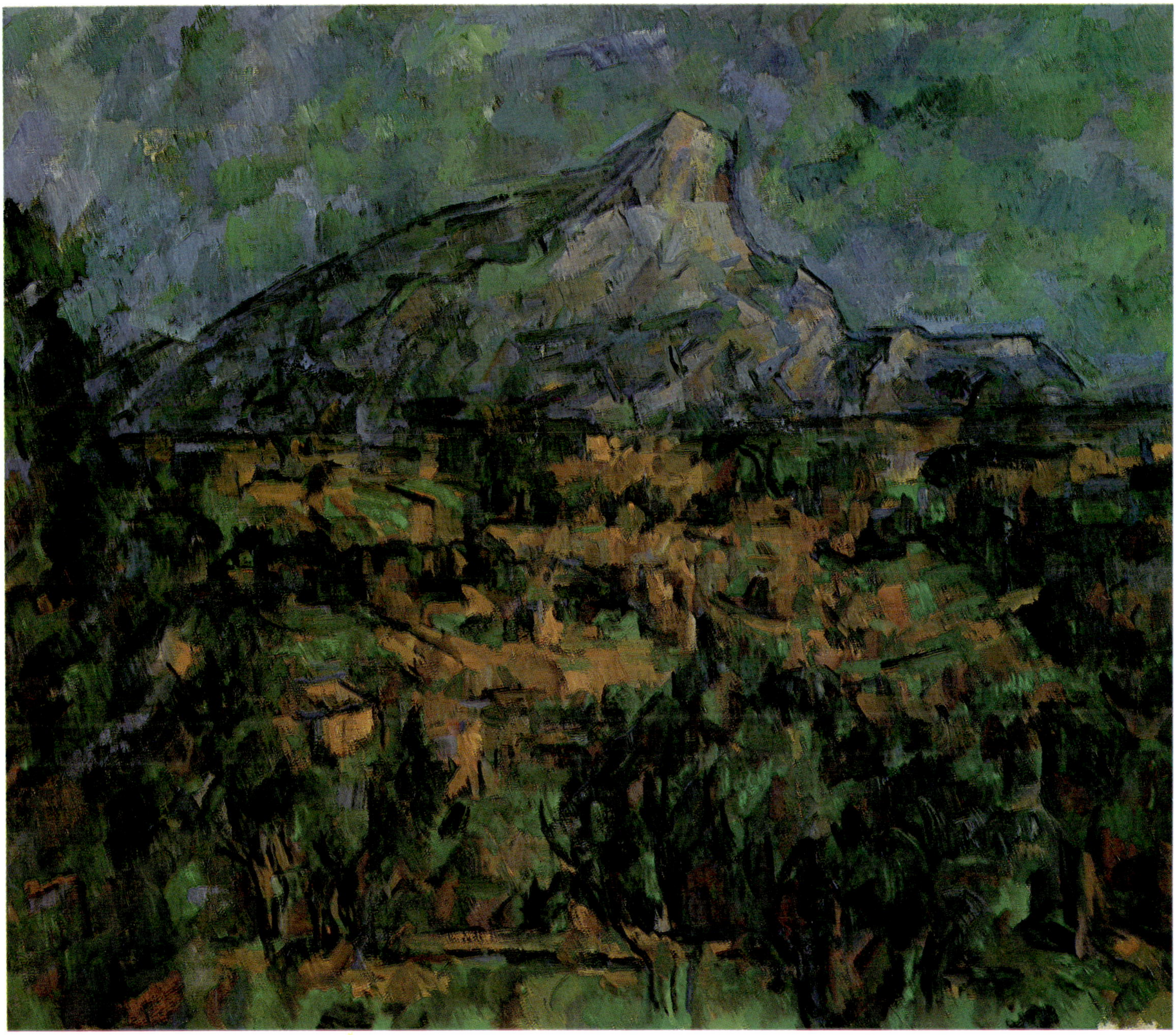

Claude Monet

(Paris 1840–Giverny 1926)

The elder son of a grocer, Monet was born in Paris, but grew up in Le Havre. There he met Eugène Boudin, who was the first to persuade him to try painting out-of-doors—a revelation to Monet. His early formal art training began in 1859 in Paris at the Académie Suisse and later (1862) at the Ecole des Beaux-Arts, where he studied under Gleyre and formed friendships with Renoir, Sisley, and Bazille. During that period (1862–66) he met Courbet, Cézanne, Whistler, and Manet, under whose influence he painted his *Déjeuner sur l'herbe* (1865)—an ambitious composition of figures in an outdoor setting. In 1865–66, his paintings were exhibited in the Salon.

To avoid the Franco-Prussian War (1870), Monet went to England, where he met the dealer Durand-Ruel. He visited the Victoria and Albert Museum and National Gallery, particularly studying Turner and Constable. He returned to Paris in 1872, via Holland and Le Havre, where he painted a view of the harbor entitled *L'Impression*. Shown at the first exhibition of the Société Anonyme des Artistes-Peintres (1874), *L'Impression* prompted the scornful label "Impressionists" for painters of Monet's persuasion.

In 1878, poverty forced Monet to move to Vétheuil, where he remained for three years, before later settling permanently at Giverny in 1884. Frequent trips—in 1883 to Normandy, and with Renoir to the Côte d'Azur—provided him with fresh source material for his landscapes. He left Giverny briefly in 1886 to paint the tulip fields of Holland.

Thanks to Durand-Ruel's efforts, Monet's financial situation improved in the nineties. At this time, he worked on several important series depicting the same motif at different times of day—*Poplars* (1890–92), *Haystacks* (1890–91), *Rouen Cathedral* (1892–95), and the *Thames* (1899–1904). He completed the London series at Giverny, for once departing from his usual dependence on nature. After the turn of the century, Monet tended more and more to dissolve forms in light. His favorite subject came to be his own garden, particularly his lily pond, which inspired canvas after canvas (*Les Nymphéas*). Gradual loss of sight may have been responsible to a certain extent for the relative abstraction of Monet's late works, but the artist never abandoned his Impressionist habit of painting from nature.

Claude Monet
1840–1926

9. *Woman in a Garden,* c. 1867

Oil on canvas, 80 × 99 cm

Signed, bottom left: Claude Monet

Hermitage Museum, inv. no. 6505

Provenance: Paul-Eugène Lecadre collection, Sainte-Adresse; 1880, Meunier collection, Sainte-Adresse; Lebas collection, Paris; 1893, Durand-Ruel Gallery, Paris; 1899, P. Shchukin collection, Moscow; 1912, S. Shchukin collection, Moscow; 1918, First Museum of Modern Western Painting, Moscow; 1923, Museum of Modern Western Art, Moscow; since 1930, Hermitage, Leningrad.

This picture was painted on the estate of Monet's aunt, Madame Lecadre, in Sainte-Adresse, near Le Havre. Today the estate is inside the city's borders. The location is confirmed by the label on the back of the painting from the Durand-Ruel Gallery, where S. Shchukin purchased it, and by the grandson of Lady (Jeanne-Marguerite) Lecadre, who was married to Monet's cousin.

It is known that at his father's request, Monet parted with Camille, his future wife, and spent the summer of 1867 in isolation at Sainte-Adresse. *Woman in a Garden* was probably created at that very period—very likely at the same time as the Louvre's *Garden in Bloom*, which depicts another part of the same garden, adjacent to the house. Although both canvases are not dated, the Louvre considers *Garden in Bloom* to have been painted in 1866. Daniel Wildenstein's catalogue also assigns this date to both paintings. However, Wildenstein published Monet's letter of June 25, 1867, to Bazille, which refers to the above landscapes: ". . . I've done a lot of pictures, some twenty canvases in all—magnificent sea views and figures, and gardens, and what not." *Terrace at Sainte-Adresse* (Metropolitan Museum of Art, New York), which was dated 1867 by Monet, became the central work of this group.

The methods used by the artist in painting this canvas are close to those used for *Woman in a Garden,* and the heroine of the Hermitage composition is also shown in the center. X-ray analysis of *Woman in a Garden* has revealed a male figure on the right that was later painted over. Rewald dates the painting c. 1866.

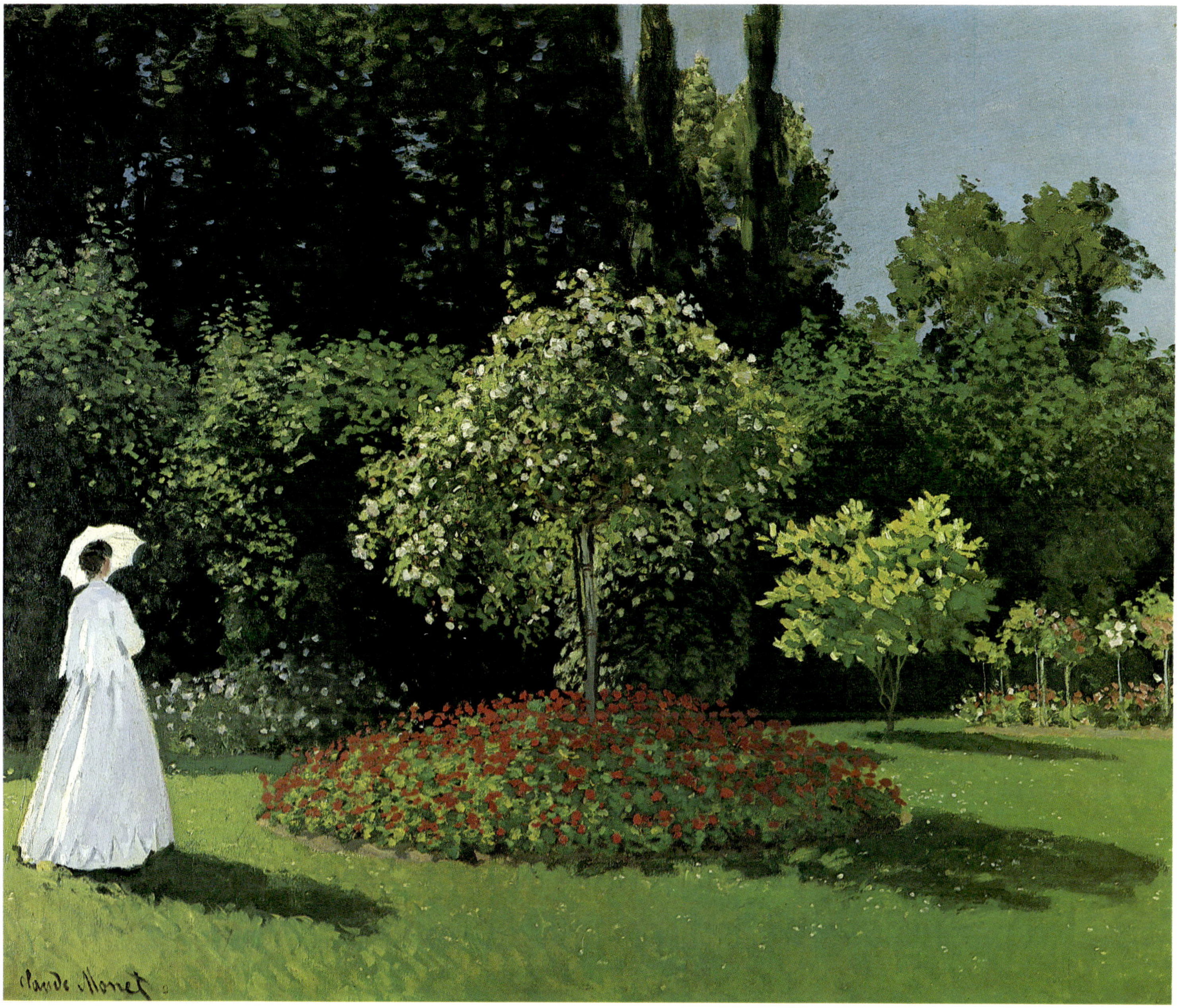
Claude Monet

Claude Monet
1840–1926

10. *Corner of the Garden at Montgeron,*
1876

Oil on canvas, 172 × 193 cm

Signed, bottom right: Cl. M.

Hermitage Museum, inv. no. 9152

Provenance: Ernest Hoschede collection, Montgeron; 1878, J. B. Faure collection, Paris (purchased from Hoschede for 50 francs in an auction); 1907, Durand-Ruel Gallery, Paris; 1907, Morozov collection, Moscow (bought for 40,000 francs); 1918, Second Museum of Modern Western Art, Moscow; 1923, Museum of Modern Western Art, Moscow; since 1948, Hermitage, Leningrad.

Together with *Pond at Montgeron* (also in the Hermitage), this painting belonged to a series of canvases that decorated the home of Ernest Hoschede in Montgeron. In spite of a widely held belief, these landscapes are not a pair, as they differ in composition. Although it is unknown how the entire series must have appeared at the time, the group also included *The Turkeys* (Louvre) and *The Chase* (Charles Durand-Ruel collection, Paris). The two latter canvases had the same height as the Hermitage ones but a different width.

Hoschede was one of the few patrons who supported the Impressionists during their intense struggle for recognition. Monet spent the autumn of 1876 in the Hoschede Château de Rottembourg in Montgeron. Contrary to his usual manner of working at the time, the *Corner of the Garden at Montgeron* was painted indoors and employed a preliminary sketch, which now belongs to the Nelson Harris collection, USA (Wildenstein, no. 417).

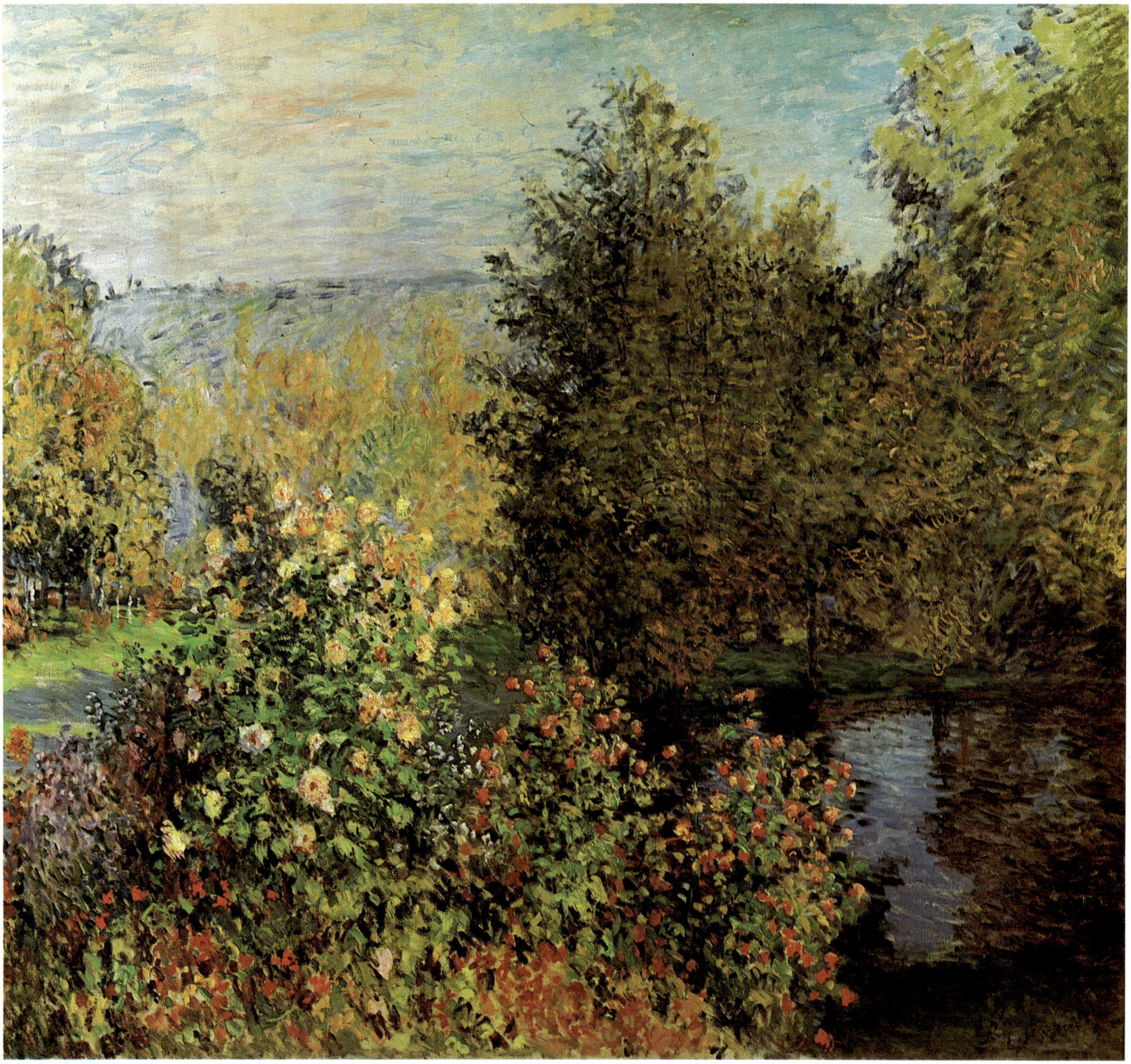

Claude Monet
1840–1926

11. *Pond at Montgeron,* c. 1876

Oil on canvas, 173 × 193 cm

Signed, bottom right: Cl. M.

Hermitage Museum, inv. no. 6562

Provenance: Ernest Hoschede collection, Paris; A. Vollard Gallery; from 1907, I. Morozov collection (purchased for 10,000 francs); 1918, Second Museum of Modern Western Painting, Moscow; 1923, Museum of Modern Western Art, Moscow; since 1931, Hermitage, Leningrad.

During the ten years that passed between the painting of *Woman in a Garden* and *Pond at Montgeron*, Impressionism acquired a range of expressive means that enabled the painters to create with a new artistic language and unique vocabulary used consistently in this painting. Here, the painter has rejected the scale formerly used to determine the importance of an object. In this picture, an ordinary pond with its low banks covered with greenery—nothing special—was now painted on a very large canvas, and the objects shown by the painter are important not because of their beautifully depicted contours, but because of their role in the general rhythm of life.

The colorful pattern of the painting nearly conceals the figures: a man resting on the bank and a lady with a fishing rod nearby. The latter figure depicted is most probably Alice, Ernest Hoschede's wife, who later became Monet's second wife. As Claude Monet was trying to depict his momentary impression in this painting, he did not use distinctive contours or small details; instead, he employed other means to relay to the spectator an image of a colorful, beautiful scene.

Together with *Corner of the Garden at Montgeron*, the canvas was part of the decorative series ordered by Ernest Hoschede for his house in Montgeron. For the *Pond* and the companion painting, Monet used a preliminary outdoor sketch, which now belongs to a private collection (Wildenstein, *Monet*, no. 419). Either the sketch or the painting was included in the Third Exhibition of Impressionists under the name of *Mare à Montgeron*.

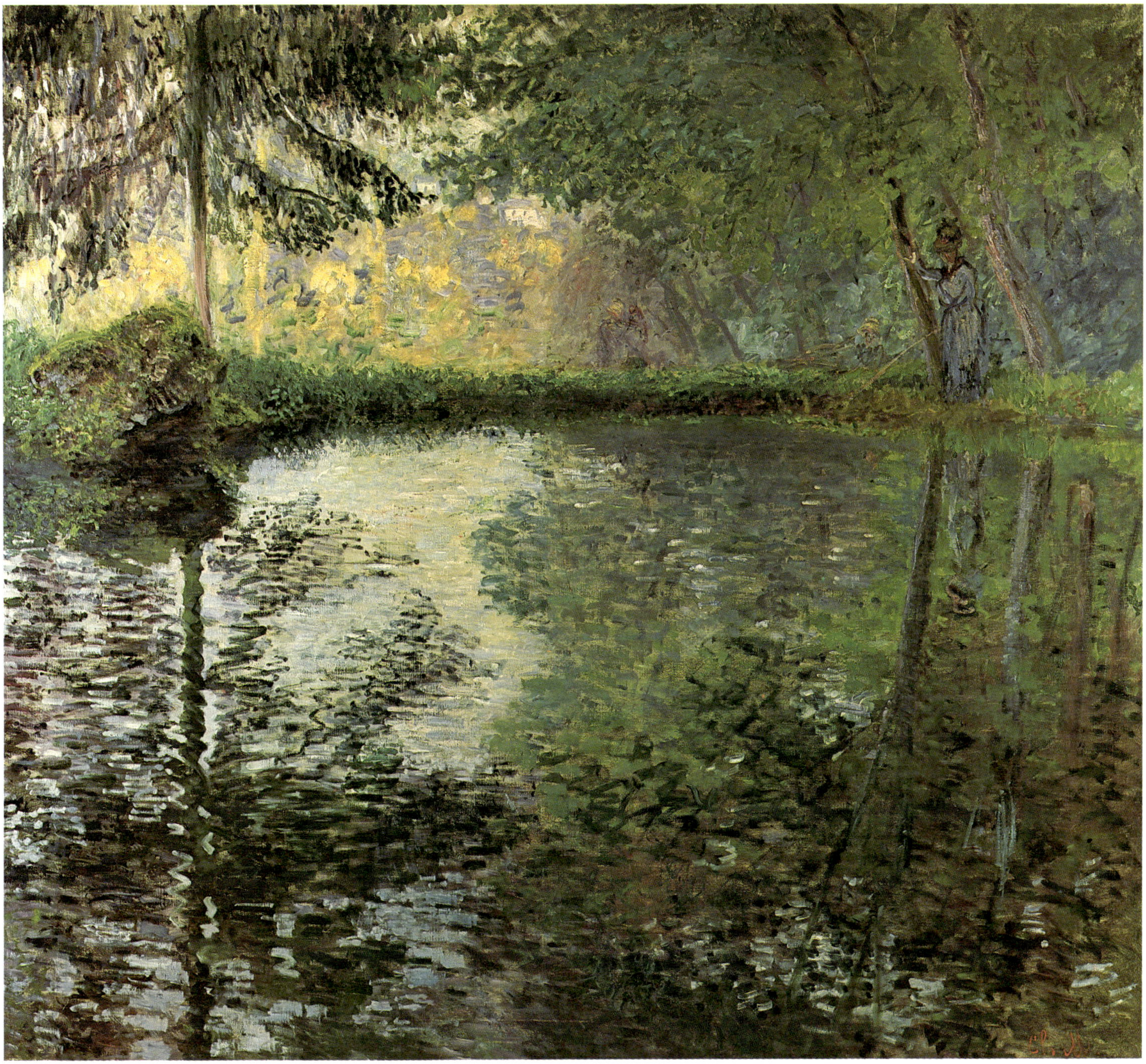

Pierre Auguste Renoir
1841–1919

12. *Bathing in the Seine (La Grenouillère),*

1868

Oil on canvas, 59 × 80 cm

Signed, bottom left: Renoir

Pushkin Museum, inv. no. 3407

Provenance: 1908, Vollard Gallery, Paris; 1908, I. Morozov collection, Moscow; 1918, Second Museum of Modern Western Painting, Moscow; 1923, Museum of Modern Western Art, Moscow; since 1948, Pushkin Museum, Moscow.

This picture depicts a small restaurant called La Grenouillère, which was a meeting place frequented by the Impressionists on the Seine between Chatou and Bougival. Renoir often represented this picturesque locale, painting it from various angles. Vollard quotes Renoir as saying that in 1868 he painted many different views of La Grenouillère (A. Vollard, *Sluchaige, Cézannea, Degasa, Renoira,* Warszawa, 1962, p. 204). On the basis of this evidence, Meier Graefe dated the Pushkin Museum painting 1868. Venturi, Rouart, and Rewald thought that the picture was painted in September 1869, about the time of a similar landscape by Claude Monet. The landscapes of both men belong to Impressionism's earliest phase.

La Grenouillère is described by Guy de Maupassant in his story *Ivette.* In 1869, Monet wrote to Bazille, ". . . I am dreaming of a picture, the swimming area of La Grenouillère, for which I have some bad sketches, but it is a dream. Renoir, who is spending two months with me, also wants to do this picture" (G. Poulain, *Bazille et ses amies,* Paris, 1932, p. 161). His project was fulfilled in his painting *Argenteuil: River and Trees* (private collection, USA) and by Renoir in a painting in the Pushkin collection, *La Grenouillère.* According to K.S. Champa, the Moscow painting is the first result of Renoir and Monet working together on the same subject. Renoir made another version of *La Grenouillère* together with Monet (collection of O. Reinhart am Römerholz, Winterthur) and yet another version (National Museum, Stockholm). Renoir returned to this scene again in 1879 (*A la Grenouillère,* Paris, Louvre).

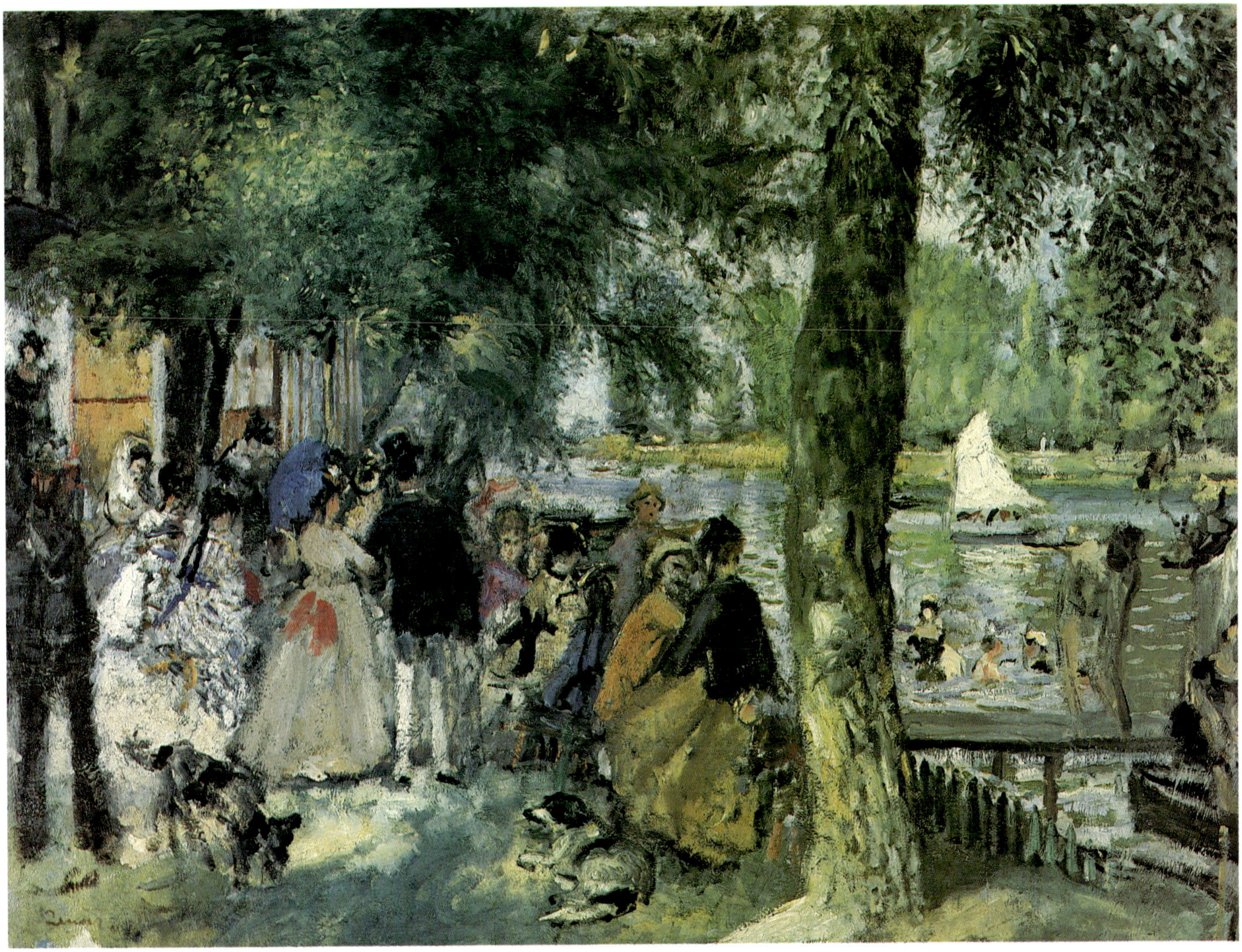

Pierre Auguste Renoir
1841–1919

13. *Lady in Black,*
 c. 1876

Oil on canvas, 63 × 53 cm

Signed, middle right: A. Renoir

Hermitage Museum, inv. no. 6506

Provenance: S. Shchukin collection, Moscow; 1891, First Museum of Modern Western Painting, Moscow; 1923, Museum of Modern Western Art, Moscow; since 1930, Hermitage, Leningrad.

While the identity of the sitter in this painting is not quite clear, some evidence exists that the woman portrayed is Mme. Hartmann, wife of a well-known music publisher. François Daulte, author of the complete catalogue of Renoir paintings, believes that *Lady in Black* was "Wonderful Anna," a prominent Montmartre model, who was also a model for Renoir's *Bathers* (Pushkin Museum) and for Monet's *Nana* (Kunsthalle, Hamburg). Although one cannot deny a certain resemblance, it is more probable that this is some other model who remains unidentified. Monet has represented the figure's purely visual and psychological characteristics and has also set as his task an investigation of the artistic possibilities of various shades of black color. Daulte dates the canvas to 1876.

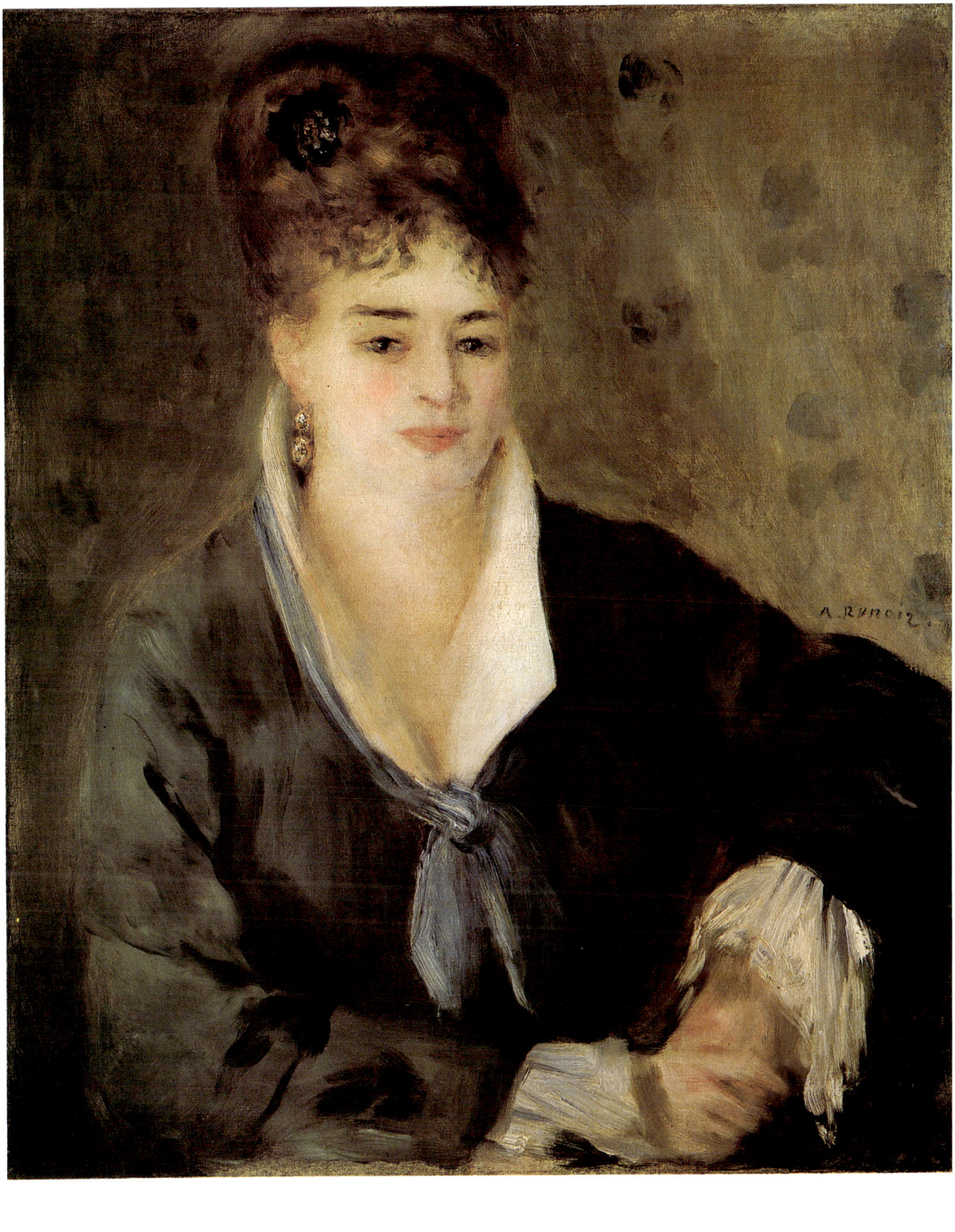
A. Renoir.

Pierre Auguste Renoir
1841–1919

14. *Portrait of the Actress Jeanne Samary*, 1878

Oil on canvas, 173 × 103 cm

Signed and dated, bottom left: Renoir, 78

Hermitage Museum, inv. no. 9003

Provenance: 1879, Durand-Ruel Gallery (bought from the artist for 1,500 francs); Prince Polignac collection, Paris; 1897, Durand-Ruel Gallery again (bought from Prince Polignac for 4,000 francs); 1898, de la Salle collection, Paris; Bernheim-Jeune Gallery, Paris; M. Morozov collection, Moscow; 1910, Tretyakov Gallery, Moscow (gift of Morozov's widow); 1925, Museum of Modern Western Art, Moscow; since 1948, Hermitage, Leningrad.

This monumental portrait is of Jeanne Samary (1857–1890), a prominent Comédie Française actress known for her roles as servants and soubrettes in Molière's plays. The portrait was painted for the 1879 Salon, where it was displayed together with another of Renoir's paintings—*Portrait of Madame Charpentier and Her Children* (Metropolitan Museum of Art, New York). Jeanne Samary is depicted in the dress she wore while visiting the Charpentiers, where it is likely that the painter met her. The portrait did not bring Renoir the success he had hoped for in the 1879 Salon largely because it was poorly displayed in the dark near the ceiling. Guismas, in his survey of the Salon exhibition, maliciously suggested that the organizers display the paintings on the ceiling. In addition, without the painter's knowledge and immediately before the Salon opening, the painting was mistakenly covered with a thick layer of varnish. The varnish layer was removed in the 1960s by a Hermitage expert.

According to the painter's son Jean, the parents of the actress (who were Renoir's neighbors) admired Renoir's work. One day they asked him to paint their daughter if he needed a model. The work was painted in a studio on the Rue Saint-Georges, and Renoir very much enjoyed doing this portrait. It is said that the artist was so eager to start painting that he sometimes forgot to say "Hello" to his model. Later in his life, the painter said about the actress, who died at an early age: "What a charming girl. What skin! It looks as if it were illuminated from inside."

Renoir's best pictures are those in which he knew his model intimately and painted her on more than one occasion. The Hermitage painting is an example, for it was the fifth portrait by Renoir of the actress. The first four date from 1877: two round medallions (Daulte, nos. 230 and 231) and two important paintings that rank among Renoir's outstanding portraits—one in the Pushkin Museum (Daulte, no. 229) and the other in the Comédie Française (Daulte, no. 228). In 1878, Renoir again painted a small portrait of Jeanne Samary, in all probability just prior to starting the large canvas in the Hermitage collection (Switzerland, private collection, Daulte, no. 277).

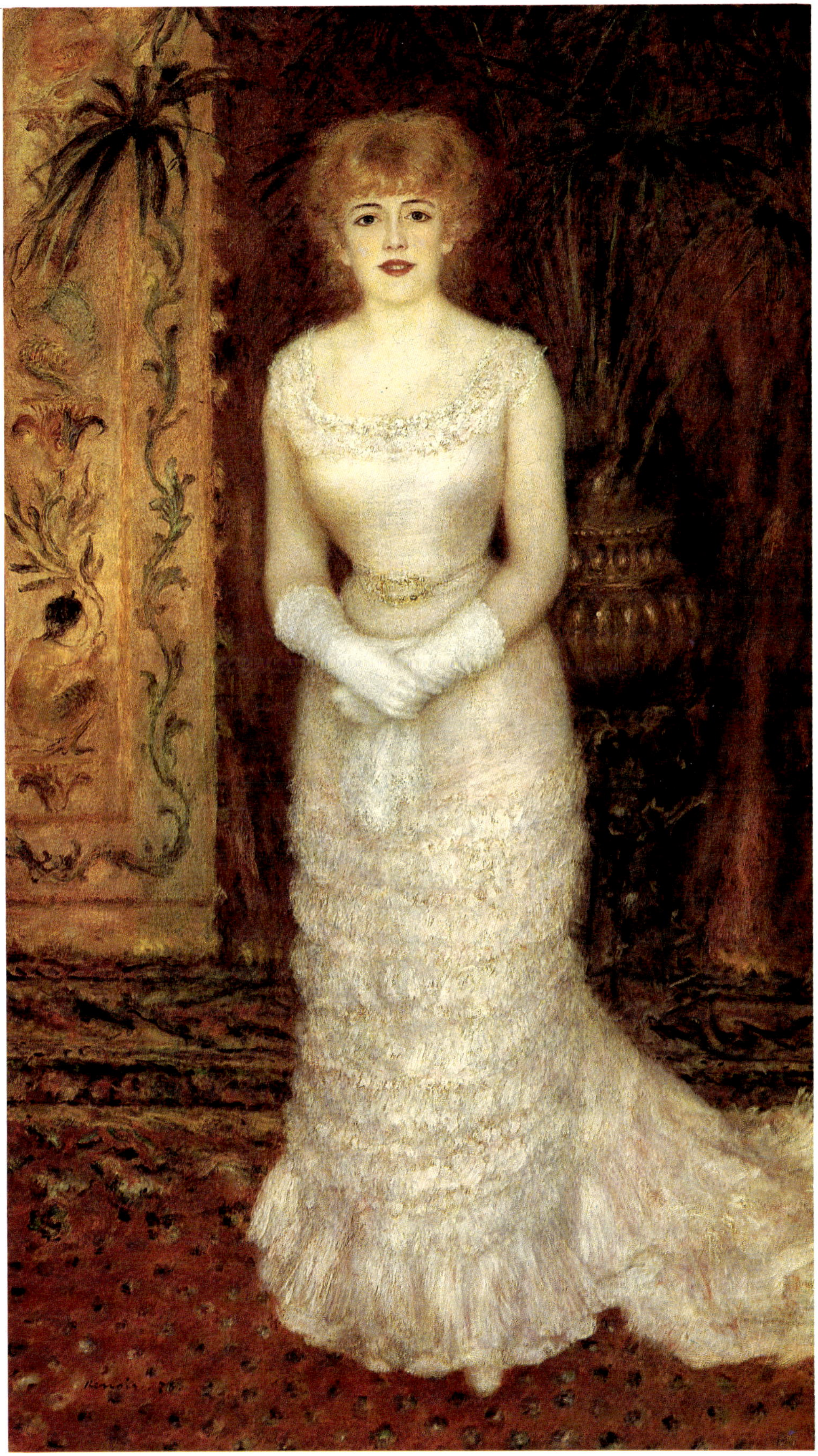

Paul Gauguin

(Paris 1848–
Marquesas Islands 1903)

Gauguin's early years included a childhood with his family in Peru, world travel with the merchant marine, and a job as a stockbroker's employee, which brought him prosperity but not satisfaction. He started painting in the 1870s first as a hobby, then as an obsession. Soon after he turned seriously to painting, he met Pissarro and Cézanne, and he exhibited with the Impressionists by the early 1880s. Restless from borrowing from and then discarding styles of Pissarro, Seurat, Degas, and others, Gauguin became anxious for inspiration and an authoritative new image. He went to Brittany in 1886, which became a primary source of inspiration. In 1887, he traveled to Martinique, and in 1888 he experienced an ill-starred relationship with van Gogh in Arles before returning to Brittany.

In Brittany, Gauguin pursued his stylistic researches, deriving inspiration from Japanese prints and English illustrations by Randolph Caldecott and Kate Greenaway. The most important new source of ideas was the much younger Emile Bernard, with whom Gauguin conceived what came to be known as the "Synthetist" style: "a synthesis of form and color derived from observation of the dominant element only" (Gauguin's words). Subsequently the two artists quarreled, both taking credit for the invention of Synthetism.

Through his friendship with the even younger Sérusier, Gauguin became the "messiah" of the new generation of artists, particularly the "Nabis," Bonnard, Vuillard, and Maurice Denis. But Gauguin's revolutionary vision found little favor with buyers, and he left for Tahiti in search of an Eden more primitive and more tropical than Brittany. There followed a succession of dazzling pictures, primitive but highly sophisticated in their eclecticism. Gauguin draws on Tahitian legends and Christian themes; quotes from Egyptian, Greek, and Japanese bas-reliefs; and borrows from artists as different as Prud'hon, Puvis de Chavannes, Manet, and Redon.

By August 1873, Gauguin was back in France—penniless. An inheritance briefly made life easier, but by September 1895, the artist was once again in Tahiti. The last period in Oceania was tragic. Gauguin eked out a living by sales to the dealer Ambroise Vollard and to his perceptive patron, Gustave Fayet, whose great group of Gauguins was bought *en bloc* by the Russian collector Shchukin. The artist fought with local officials, with his women and friends. His newborn daughter died, money from Europe repeatedly failed to arrive, and massive heart attacks nearly killed him. Yet somehow he survived to paint his large masterpiece, *Where Do We Come From? What Are We? Where Are We Going?* (1897). Gauguin hated the way missionaries were cleaning up Tahiti, and in 1901 moved to the more primitive Marquesas Islands, where he died.

Paul Gauguin
1848–1903

15. *Self-Portrait*,
1888?

Oil on canvas, 46 × 37 cm

Signed, bottom left: P. Go

Pushkin Museum, inv. no. 3264

Provenance: Bought by S. Shchukin from Fayet (?) in Paris after 1906; 1918, First Museum of Modern Western Painting, Moscow; 1923, Museum of Modern Western Art, Moscow; since 1948, Pushkin Museum, Moscow.

In April 1903, Gauguin sent three paintings, including the *Self-Portrait*, to an art collector named Gustav Fayet and informed his friend de Monfreid about it. Later, S. Shchukin bought two paintings, *Ruperupe* and *The Ford*, from Fayet. Also at this time, Shchukin bought from Fayet this *Self-Portrait*, which makes it possible to infer that the picture was sent from Tahiti in 1903. However, no evidence exists that would confirm that both cases refer to the same self-portrait. As this *Self-Portrait* does not have a date written by the artist, the opinions about the date of the work differ widely. Rewald and Sterling have dated it 1888–1890 and assigned it to the Breton period, when the artist lived in Arles. Wildenstein agreed with Sterling and dated *Self-Portrait* 1888 in his catalogue. According to Sterling, the reason for this date is based on the rounded form of the mustache shown by Gauguin in his painting *Self-Portrait with the Yellow Christ*. Wildenstein also suggested that in a letter to his brother of January 9, 1889, the artist talked about this very portrait just finished by him in Arles. Lately Cooper shared this opinion. However, the bright yellow line at the left of this work reminds us of the yellow background in many of the paintings of the Tahitian period. A similar yellow line is in the background of *Self-Portrait with a Hat*, painted during Gauguin's stay in Paris in 1893–1894 after he had returned from Tahiti. It is also interesting to note that both self-portrait canvases are the same size and have similar inscriptions on the back: "P. GO, Self-Portrait with a Hat."

To the left of the figure's head is a bright yellow band, which may be the frame of a window; to the right beyond the window is a vague outline of a pink cottage and a large red leaf. It should be noted that since this work was painted the paint layer of the portrait has become dull and the contours of the objects abraded, which makes it difficult to discern the details of the background. The existence of an apparent Tahitian landscape in the background indicates that the work was painted in Tahiti. This opinion is shared by Pertsov and probably also by Shchukin.

Nevertheless, the date of the Moscow *Self-Portrait* has still not been completely determined. Efforts have been made to refer it to the last period of the painter's life on the basis that it is similar to the *Self-Portrait* sent in 1903 to Fayet and also because the canvas is characteristic of the material Gauguin used while at the Marquesas Islands. However, these arguments are not very convincing, because Gauguin used this type of canvas at various periods during his lifetime, including during his stay in Arles in 1888. It might be more correct to date the *Self-Portrait* to 1890–1893, when the painter came to Tahiti for the first time.

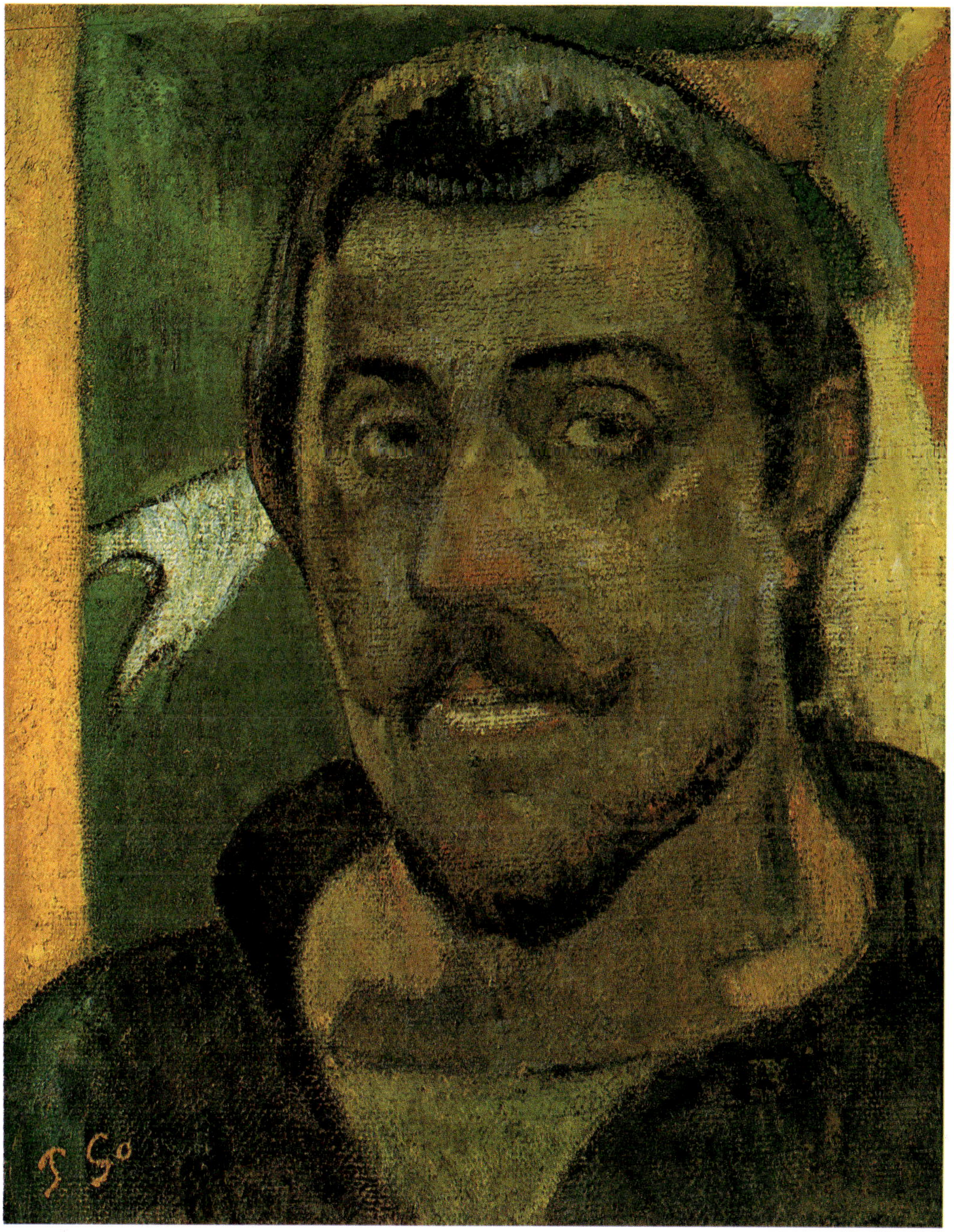
P. Go

Paul Gauguin
1848–1903

16. *The Flowers of France
(Te Tiare Farani),*
1891

Oil on canvas, 72 × 92 cm

Signed and dated, bottom left: P. Gauguin 91

Inscribed on the table, bottom right: TE TIARE FARANI

Pushkin Museum, inv. no. 3370

Provenance: This painting was at the auction of Gauguin's work in the Hôtel Drouot in Paris on February 16, 1895 (no. 24 was bought by the painter for 340 francs); c. 1906, Vollard Gallery, Paris (?); bought by I. Morozov from Vollard Gallery in 1908; 1919, Second Museum of Modern Western Painting, Moscow; 1923, Museum of Modern Western Art, Moscow, no. 298; since 1948, Pushkin Museum, Moscow.

The year 1891, in which the painting was dated, was a decisive year in Gauguin's personal and professional life. This was the year he left France and went to Tahiti. The treatment of the still life—a tabletop with a pitcher of large flowers—betrays the influence of Cézanne's lessons; the compositional structure of the picture and the arrangement of the figures cut by the frame reveal a debt to the traditions of Monet and Degas.

The mood of *The Flowers of France* is very similar to the one in Monet's *Breakfast in the Studio*. There is a direct connection between the figure of the Tahitian looking out of the picture at the view and the pose of the young man in a straw hat bent over a table in the work by Monet, the central figure in the painting *Breakfast in the Studio*. If we consider Monet's version as an explanation of the young man's internal feelings, then we see that it fully corresponds to Gauguin's own mood when he made his decision to leave Europe and settle in Polynesia. In the painting, the young man is standing at a map, evidently getting ready for traveling. In this way, the nostalgic feelings prompted in the painting are not just reminiscences of home while living abroad, but are also a last farewell to the painter's former idols, Cézanne, Degas, and Monet, whose work delighted Gauguin. In Gauguin's notebooks, there is a study of a figure of a young Tahitian man in a hat. A similar face of a Tahitian in a hat can be found on a sheet of paper with sketches (Rewald, no. 36).

The Flowers of France is one of the first of Gauguin's paintings in which he uses a Tahitian phrase revealing its actual meaning: "Te Tiare Farani" is translated as *Flowers of France* (Bouge, 1956, p. 164, no. 61; Danielsson, 1967, p. 233, no. 77).

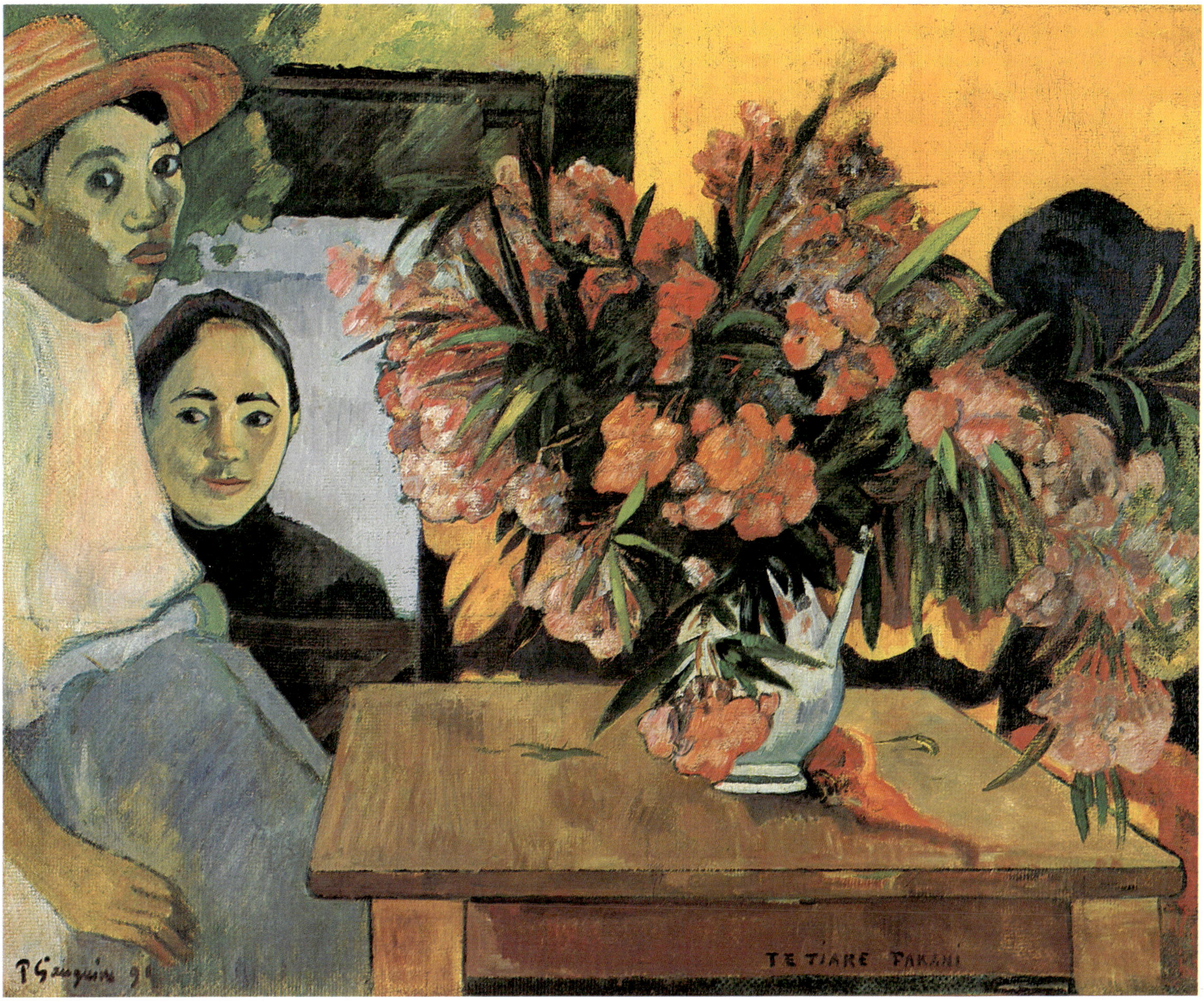
P Gauguin 91
TE TIARE FARANI

Paul Gauguin
1848–1903

17. *Her Name Is Vaïraumati (Vaïraumati Tei Oa),*
1892

Oil on canvas, 91 × 68 cm

Signed and dated, bottom left: Paul Gauguin 92 Tahiti

Inscribed, bottom center: Vaïraumati tei oa

Pushkin Museum, inv. no. 3266

Provenance: 1895, sale of Gauguin's pictures before his second trip to Tahiti, no. 15 (bought by the painter himself); Shchukin collection, Moscow; 1918, First Museum of Modern Western Painting, Moscow; 1923, Museum of Modern Western Art, Moscow; since 1948, Pushkin Museum, Moscow.

This work dates from Gauguin's first Tahitian period when the artist fell under the spell of old Maori legends. He relates the legend of the God Horo and the beautiful Vaïraumati in his 1924 book, *Noa Noa*. While providing an illustration for this legend, the artist fills the picture with new meaning.

Vaïraumati is sitting on a couch before a table laden with fruit. Beside her, enchanted by her beauty, stands Horo, who has descended from heaven. This scene is presented against a Tahitian landscape with an ancient stone sculpture in the background. While the ancient artist recreated an episode from the same legend of Horo and Vaïraumati, which figures in the picture twice, the scene in the foreground appears to be a modern interpretation of this myth. Gauguin has depicted Vaïraumati in the guise of a contemporary Tahitian girl, as evidenced by the smoking cigarette she holds in her hand. In his preface to *Noa Noa*, Charles Morice noted Gauguin's tendency to endow Tahitian people with divine qualities. To make his model look like a goddess, Gauguin depicted her in the pose of a priestess from an Egyptian frieze found in the British Museum, a photograph of which he had brought with him to Tahiti. In the same year, that frieze inspired him to paint *Te Matete*, in which several female figures are shown in the pose of Vaïraumati.

Another version of the Moscow canvas exists that shows Vaïraumati, but without Horo or the Tahitian idol in the background, titled *Te As No Arsois (The Origin of Arsois)*, in which the woman holds a budding flower in her left hand, a symbol of the clan's origin. According to Rewald, the model for this version was Tehura, Gauguin's first Tahitian wife, who is the same model apparently depicted in the Moscow picture.

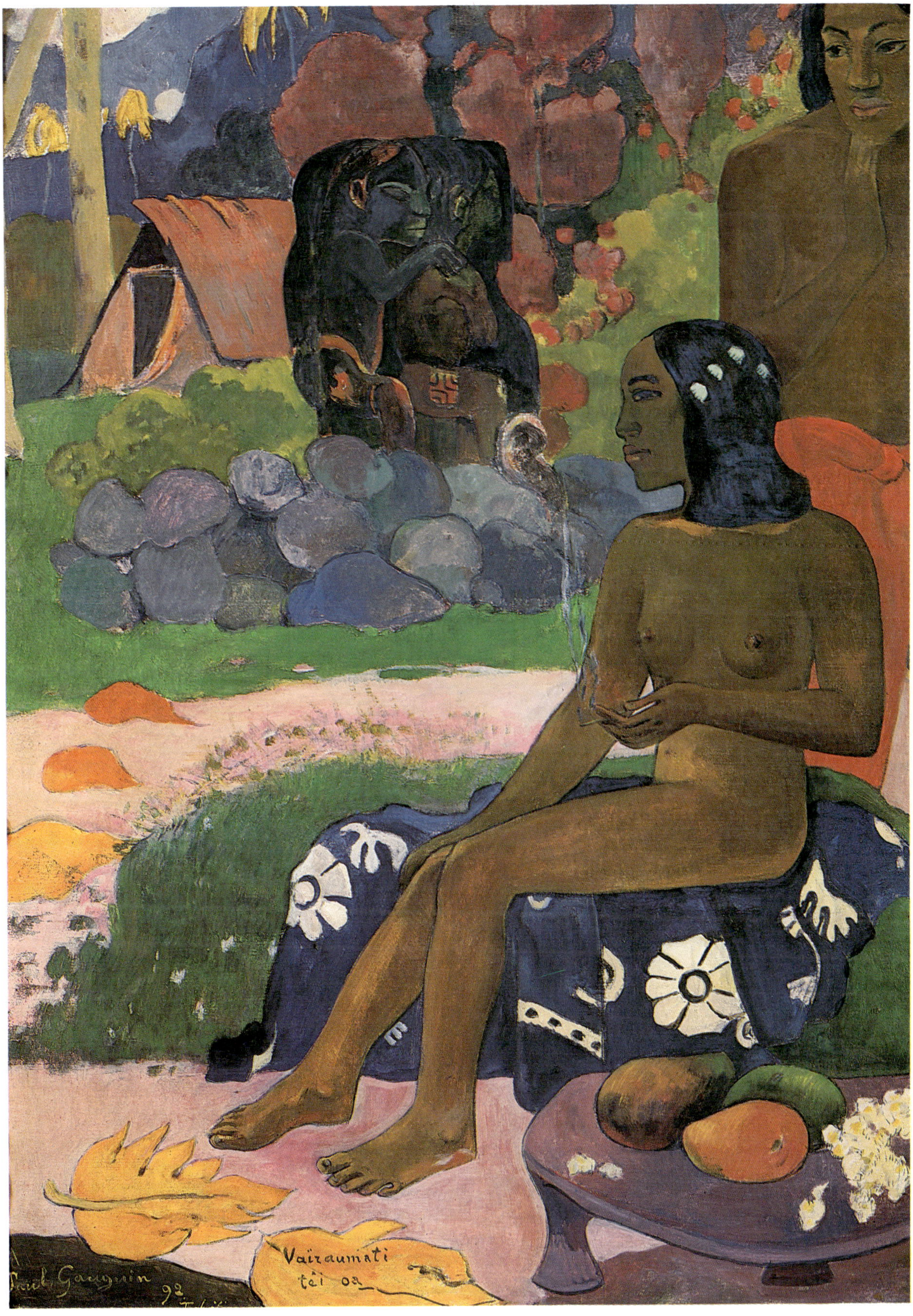
Paul Gauguin 92
Vaïraumati
tei oa

Paul Gauguin
1848–1903

18. *The Dead Tree (Matamoe)*, 1892

Oil on canvas, 115 × 86 cm

Inscribed, signed and dated, bottom right: MATAMOE, P. Gauguin 92

Pushkin Museum, inv. no. 3369

Provenance: This painting was at the auction of Gauguin's paintings in the Hôtel Drouot in 1895, no. 4, bought by A. Cegen for 480 francs; from 1906, Vollard Gallery, Paris; 1907, bought from Vollard by I. Morozov together with *Conversation* (Hermitage) for 15,000 francs; 1919–1923, Second Museum of Modern Western Painting, Moscow; 1923–1948, Museum of Modern Western Art, Moscow; since 1948, Pushkin Museum, Moscow.

The Dead Tree is one of the best works painted by Gauguin during his first stay in Tahiti. The central figure of the painting is a young Tahitian man with an axe held up behind his head, as if chopping wood, a scene Gauguin witnessed one morning in Tahiti while walking along the shore. It is described in his book *Noa Noa*: "It is morning. In the sea near the shore, I see a canoe. There is a woman in the canoe and a man on the shore. The man is almost naked. There is a high cocoa palm near the man. With an elegant movement, the man raises an axe with both hands. The axe shines brightly against a silvery sky and then leaves a deep mark on the dead tree."

It is probable that Gauguin started this painting in 1891 after he saw this picturesque scene. The picture *Tahitian with Axe* depicted everything described in *Noa Noa* and was done before the Pushkin Museum canvas. The figure of the man with an axe was introduced into the Moscow picture without any changes. In spite of the fact that the painter witnessed this scene himself, the pose was borrowed from a photograph of a Parthenon frieze that the artist brought with him to Tahiti (Dorival, *Sources of the Art of Gauguin*, 1951, p. 121). The pose of the Tahitian youth with an axe is the same as one of the figures on the Parthenon frieze. Gauguin also made a preliminary drawing of the figure, which was published by Morice (Morice, *Paul Gauguin*, 1919, p. 128).

For a long time the word "matamoe" written in the lower right corner of the painting has provoked argument. Some have tried to explain that Gauguin misspelled the Tahitian word *matamua*. In his list of Tahitian inscriptions made by Gauguin, Bouge translated it as *étrangers*. However, the word *matamoe* was also used in another inscription made by Gauguin, "Arii Matamoe," on a canvas depicting the execution of a Tahitian prince—a Tahitian version of the story of Christ. In the catalogue for the Durand-Ruel exhibition in 1893, Gauguin translated it himself as "mort du roi," while the name of this painting was translated as *Mort*. Danielsson gave the most convincing explanation of the inscription "matamoe" by translating the Tahitian word as "death." In his diary, Gauguin wrote how early one morning he went with a Tahitian youth to cut trees and had a feeling that together with the tree he destroyed in himself all the vestiges of a civilized man. This is a more plausible explanation of the word *mort*. The Moscow painting should therefore be considered not just as a "landscape with peacocks" (one of the title variations for this work), but as a symbolic canvas announcing the birth of a new man—Gauguin in Tahiti.

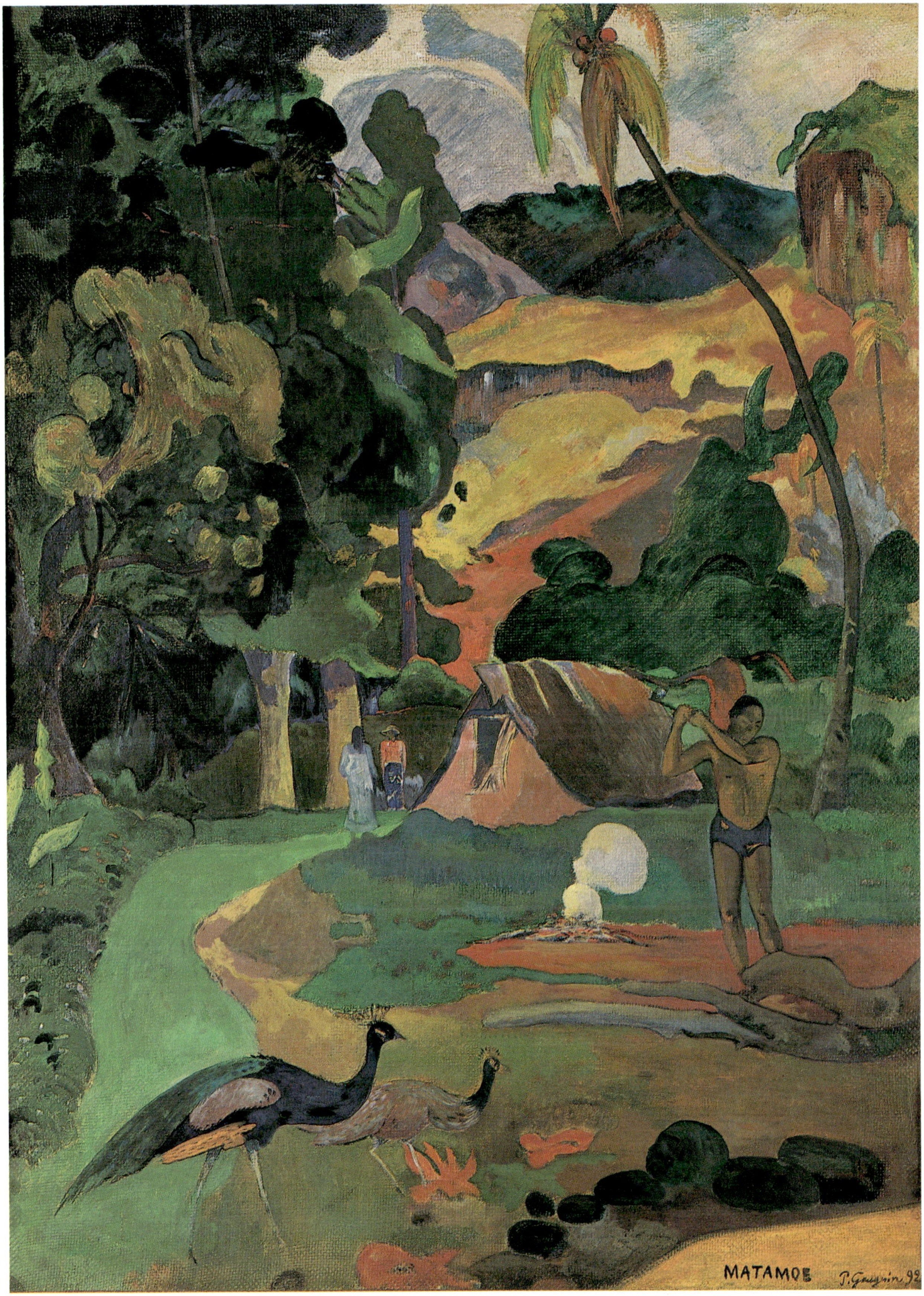
MATAMOE
P. Gauguin 92

Paul Gauguin
1848–1903

19. *Are You Jealous?*
(Aha oe feii?),
1892

Oil on canvas, 66 × 89 cm

Signed and dated, bottom center: P. Gauguin 92

Inscribed, bottom left: Aha oe feii?

Pushkin Museum, inv. no. 3269

Provenance: 1895, sale of Gauguin's paintings in the Hôtel Drouot, no. 19 (bought by Leclanché for 500 francs); 1908, Shchukin collection, Moscow; 1918, First Museum of Modern Western Painting, Moscow; 1923, Museum of Modern Western Art, Moscow; since 1948, Pushkin Museum, Moscow.

Painted during Gauguin's first Tahitian period, this picture is one of the first examples of his use of a synthetic method of depicting Tahitian landscape and figures. While working on the canvas, Gauguin used a scene from Tahitian life that he later described in the pages of his book *Noa Noa*: "On the shore, two sisters are lying after bathing, in the graceful poses of resting animals; they speak of yesterday's love and tomorrow's victories. The recollection causes them to quarrel: 'What, Are You Jealous?' " Gauguin tried to write the last phrase in Tahitian on the painting itself—*Aha oe feii.* Danielsson noticed that Gauguin misunderstood the actual meaning of the Tahitian words, which actually translate as "having a grudge against somebody." On this basis, Cooper translated the name of the Moscow painting as "Pourquoi me portes-tu rancune?" (D. Cooper in *Burlington Magazine* September 1983, p. 576, no. 19). This translation is incorrect, as Gauguin himself wanted to name the painting by using a phrase from his book *Noa Noa*: "Eh quoi? tu es jalouse!," which was the name the artist gave to the painting at the Durand-Ruel exhibition in 1893. No joke is made in the painting; the girls' poses are very precise and the central figure is borrowed from a statue of Dionysus, a photo of which Gauguin had brought with him to Tahiti. Gauguin considered this canvas very important. In his letter to Daniel de Monfreid in August 1892, he wrote that he was satisfied with the canvas and thought it significant. In December 1892, Gauguin sent several of his paintings, including this one, to an exhibition in Denmark. In a letter to his wife, he asked her not to sell it for less than 800 francs. The central figure of the Tahitian woman in a wreath of white flowers was later repeated by Gauguin in a number of canvases: *Nave Nave Moe*, 1894, included in this exhibition, no. 21; *Les Tahitiennes dans la Chambre*, 1896, also included in this exhibition as *Relax*, no. 23; *Femmes au Bord de la Rivière*, 1898; *Le Grand Bouddha*, 1899; and *L'or de Leur Corps*, 1901.

The model in the same pose is also repeated in watercolors, drawings, and etchings made by Gauguin to illustrate his book *Noa Noa* and his *Tahitian Sketchbook*.

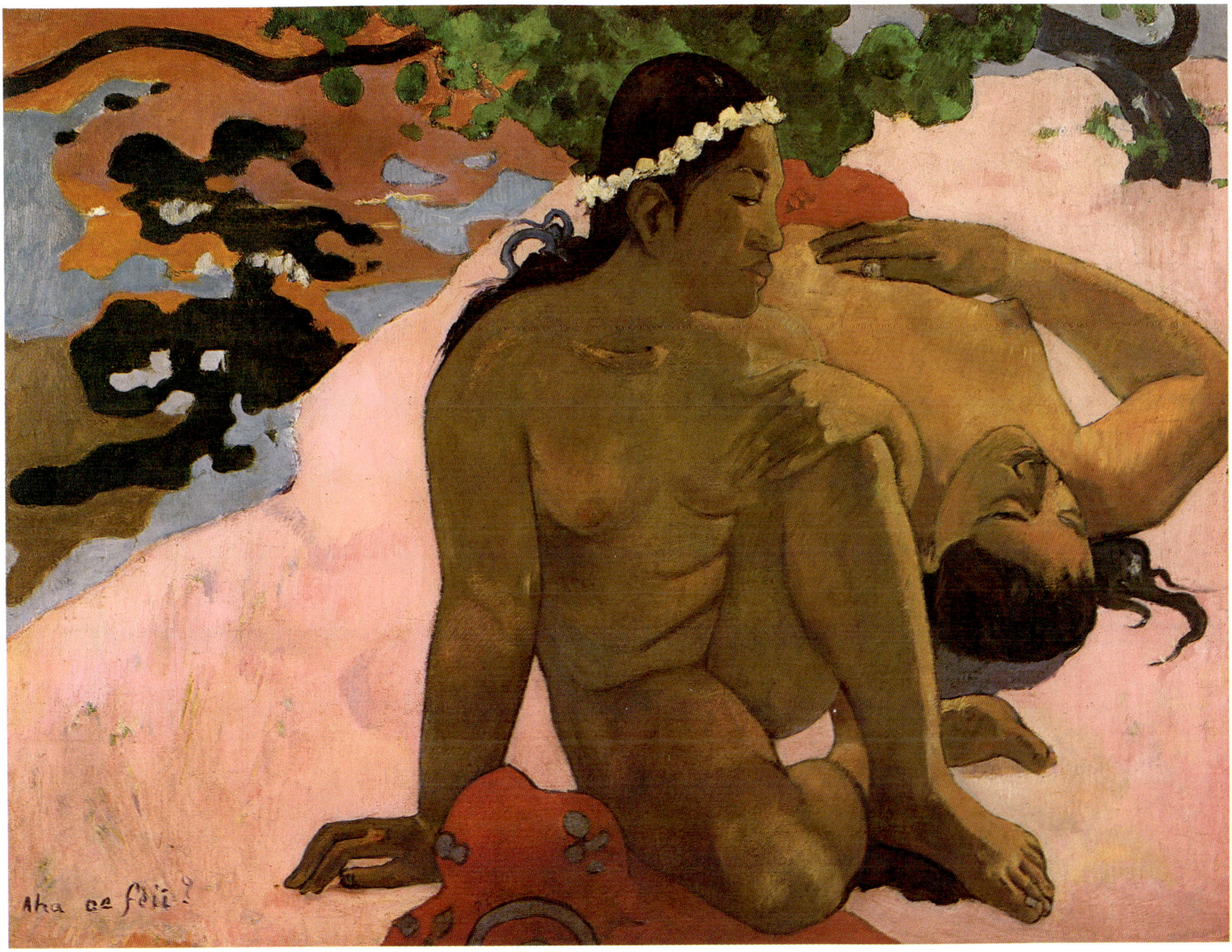
Aha oe feii?

Paul Gauguin
1848–1903

20. *Tahitian Pastoral Scene*, 1893

Oil on canvas, 86 × 113 cm

Inscribed, signed, and dated, bottom right: Pastorales tahitiennes 1893 Paul Gauguin

Hermitage Museum, inv. no.9119

Provenance: Vente Gauguin, February 18, 1895, cat. no. 5 (bought for 480 francs); Bernheim-Jeune Gallery, Paris; A. Vollard Gallery, Paris; 1908, I. Morozov collection, Moscow; 1919, Second Museum of Modern Western Painting, Moscow; 1923, Museum of Modern Western Art, Moscow; since 1948, Hermitage, Leningrad.

This painting occupies a special place among the pictures of the first Tahitian period, as Gauguin was consistently attracted to the idea of a synthesis between painting and music. In *Tahitian Pastoral Scene*, the musical theme is not only included in the plot of the painting but is used as a symbol—music reigns generally over everything living and particularly over animals. The musical theme determines the refined rhythm of linear lines in the painting, its overall solemn key, and the generalization of the background landscape, and justifies the artist's desire to saturate the canvas with color. In a letter to his friend Daniel de Monfreid (December 1892), Gauguin wrote: "I have just finished three canvases. . . . They seem to be the best, and as the first of January will be in a few days, I am going to date one of them, the best one, 1893. As an exception I gave it a French name, *Tahitian Pastoral Scene*, as I could not find an appropriate word in the language of the Kanaka. Don't know why (everything is covered with pure green veronese and similar cinnabar) it seems to me that this is an antique Holland painting or an old tapestry. How can this be explained? Anyway, all my canvases look faded."

A smaller painting called *Arearea* (D'Orsay Museum, Paris) may be considered to be a version of *Tahitian Pastoral Scene*, also painted in 1892, although earlier in the year. The landscape background of this earlier work is almost identical to that of the Hermitage canvas.

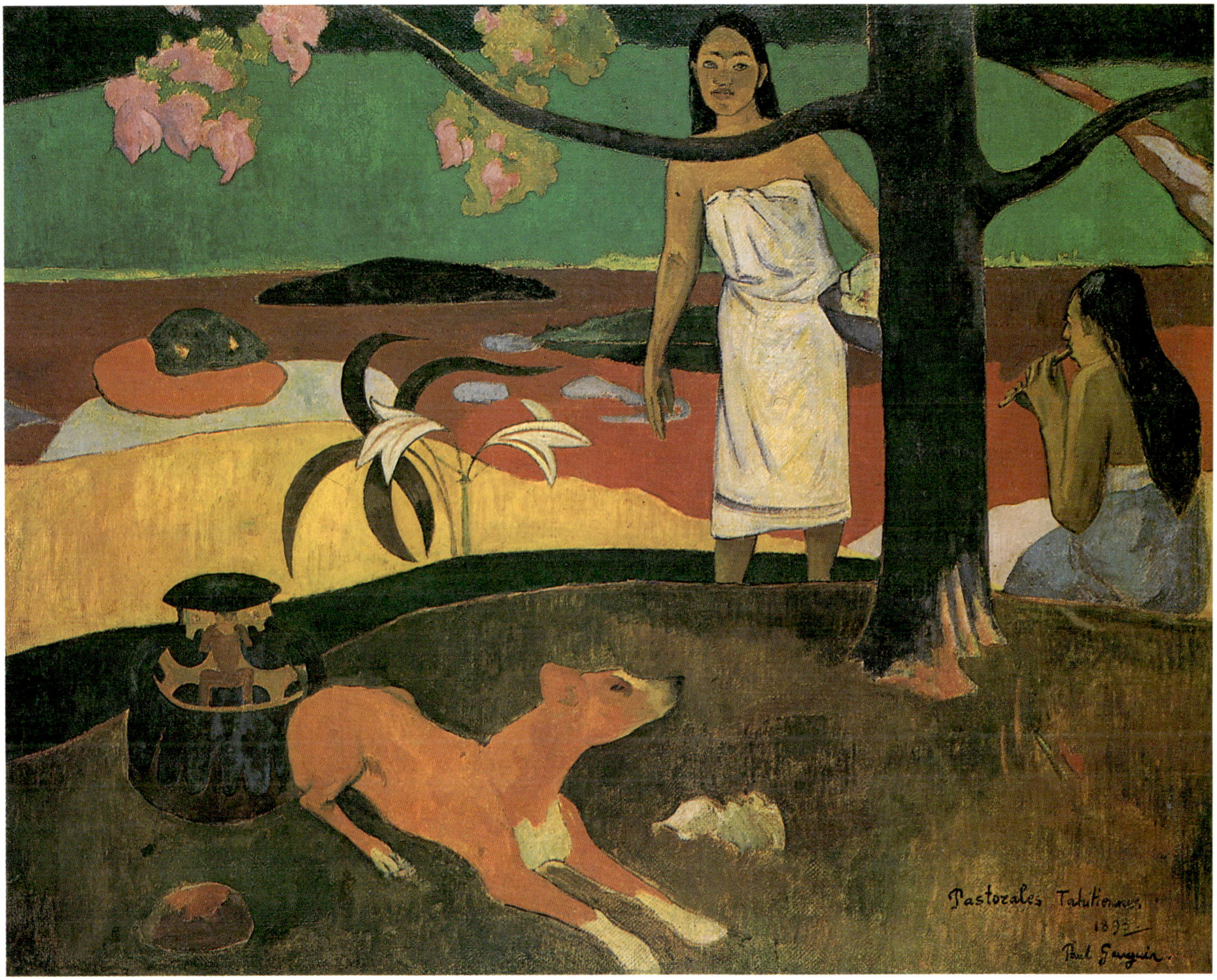
Pastorales Tahitiennes
1893
Paul Gauguin.

Paul Gauguin
1848–1903

21. *Reveries (Nave Nave Moe)*, 1894

Oil on canvas, 73 × 98 cm

Inscribed, signed, and dated, bottom left: NAVE NAVE MOE P. Gauguin 94

Hermitage Museum, inv. no. 6510

Provenance: Vente Gauguin, Paris, Hôtel Drouot, February 18, 1895, no. 23, bought by A. Schuffenecker for 430 francs at the show-sale of Gauguin's works; Dosbourg sale, Paris, November 10, 1897, lot 16 (sold for 160 francs); Prince de Wagram collection, Paris; 1907, Vollard Gallery, Paris; 1908, I. Morozov collection, Moscow (bought for 8,000 francs); 1918, Second Museum of Modern Western Painting, Moscow; 1923, Museum of Modern Western Art, Moscow; since 1931, Hermitage, Leningrad.

Eau délicieuse is the traditional name for this painting in the Hermitage collection and was derived from the 1895 catalogue of Gauguin's works compiled most likely by the painter himself for his exhibition and sale. The Tahitian name painted on the canvas is translated in various ways. Wildenstein translates it as "joie de se reposer." Bouge and Danielsson suggest more accurate alternatives: "Doux rêves," and "Delightful drowsiness" (*rêverie délicieuse*).

The painting belongs to the period between the painter's two visits to Tahiti. It was painted at the beginning of 1894, following the stained-glass panels *Nave Nave* and *Tahitian Woman in a Landscape* (D'Orsay Museum, Paris) from the end of the previous year for the painter's studio in Paris. In these panels the painter depicted a lily, which was later repeated on the right side of *Reveries*. The picture was executed in Paris as a memory of Oceania and is full of images characteristic of the first Tahitian period. Gauguin's Paris studio was filled with canvases brought with him from the tropics. The figures shown in the foreground of *Reveries* are also present in *Maori House* of 1891 (Wildenstein, no. 436). The seated nude in the center is also seen in *Are You Jealous?*, 1892 (Pushkin Museum, Wildenstein, no. 461), and the Tahitian woman standing nearby had already been shown before in three canvases from 1892 (Wildenstein, nos. 472, 473, and 474). The Tahitian "Twin God" in the upper right corner of the picture had also been shown in *Her Name is Vaïraumati*, 1892 (Wildenstein, no. 450). One can find analogous images for other details as well. In 1898 in Tahiti, Gauguin returned to the composition of *Reveries* while painting *Women on a Riverbank* (Wildenstein, no. 574).

While depicting the world of non-European beliefs, Gauguin at the same time filled his composition with Christian art symbols: An exotic lily embodies the essence of tropical nature and simultaneously symbolizes purity; the halo, unknown to the Tahitians, is a sign of virginity. The spring itself has for various peoples and at various times served as a symbol of purity. The spring and the space between the sacred stones depicted here—where ritual dances were performed in front of an idol—were integral parts of an outdoor Tahitian temple.

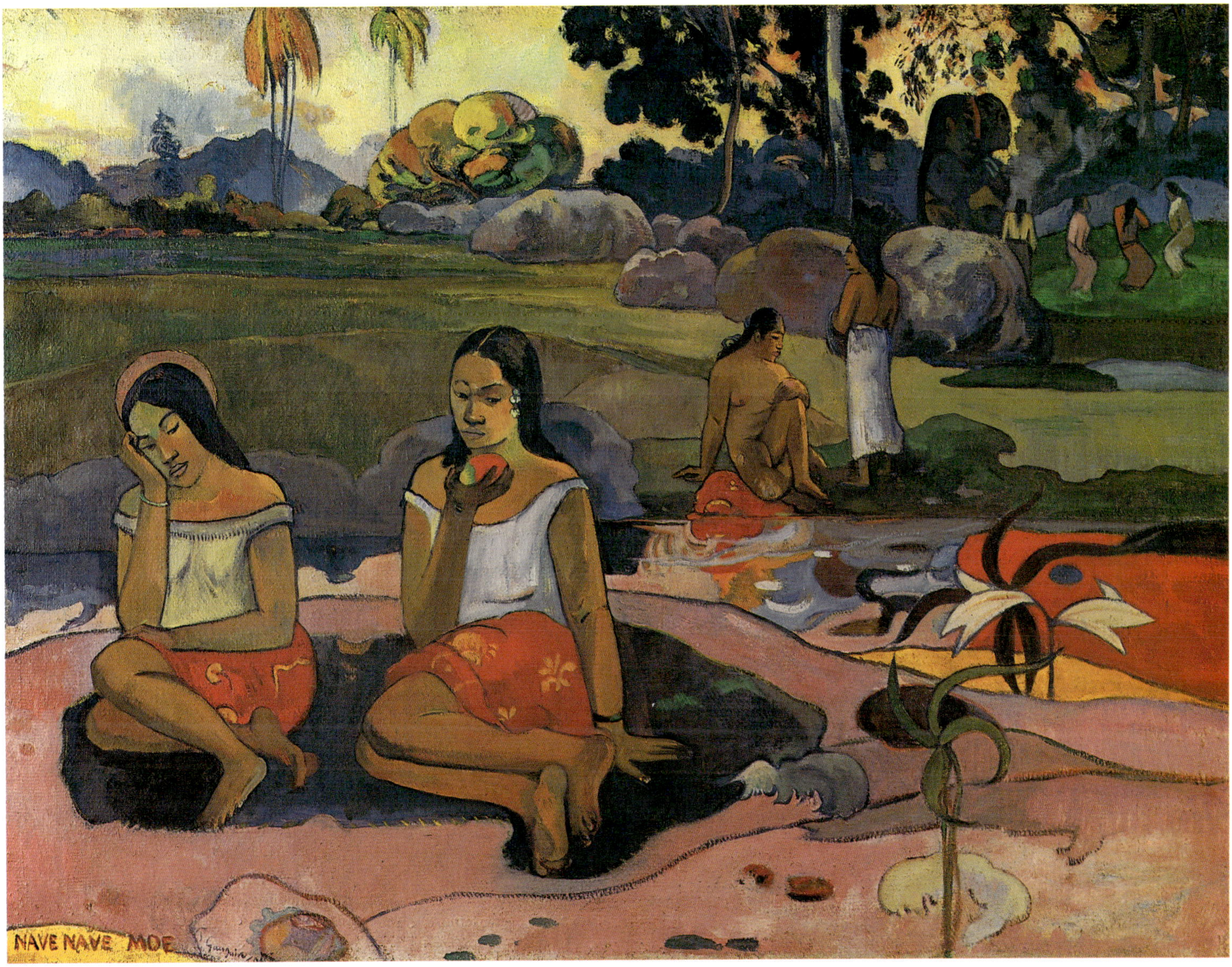
NAVE NAVE MOE

Paul Gauguin
1848–1903

22. *The Canoe (Te Vaa),*
1896

Oil on canvas, 95.5 × 131.5 cm

Inscribed, signed, and dated, bottom left:
TE VAA P. Gauguin 96

Hermitage Museum, inv. no. 9122

Provenance: M. Morozov collection, Moscow; 1903, Mrs. Morozov's collection, Moscow; 1910, Tretyakov Gallery, Moscow (gift of Morozov's widow); 1925, Museum of Modern Western Art, Moscow; since 1948, Hermitage, Leningrad.

The Canoe is the largest canvas by Gauguin represented in the Hermitage collection, and the concept behind the picture was a very important one for the painter. There is a small version of the picture that represents a single figure and is called *Poor Fisherman* (1896, Art Museum, São Paolo; Wildenstein, *Gauguin*, no. 545). The colors of the smaller canvas are not as accomplished as those in *The Canoe* in spite of the fact that the Hermitage canvas has deteriorated over time. A reference to the painting in a letter by the artist, quoted by Wildenstein in the catalogue raisonné of Gauguin's paintings, is thought to refer to the *Poor Fisherman* and can be attributed to *The Canoe* as well. ("On December 9, a group of 9 canvases was sent to the art dealer Vollard. Here are their names: . . . Sea landscape with a fisherman drinking near his boat. . . .")

The Tahitian name of the picture *Te Vaa* can be translated as "canoe." The idea was borrowed from the *Poor Fisherman* by Puvis de Chavannes (1881, D'Orsay Museum, Paris, a sketch of which is in the Pushkin Museum), a very popular painting of the time—one highly valued by Gauguin. The principal figure of *The Canoe* is reminiscent of figures depicted in ancient Egyptian art; his pose is directly related to those of figures found on the stones of Egyptian burials.

While Gauguin follows Puvis de Chavannes in depicting a family, his manner in treating the subject is quite different. Puvis' figures are divided by space. Gauguin shows them close to each other and dynamically interrelated, so much so that the figure of the Tahitian woman may be considered as having been painted "incorrectly"—the size of the figure contradicts accurate perspective. This contradiction may be partly explained by the painter's desire to construct the composition on the crossing diagonal lines of the boat and of the woman's body.

The upper part of the painting is crowned with a mountain whose mysterious profile plays the dual role of a characteristic feature of Tahitian landscape while uniting the two main figures. At the same time, the mountain acts as a symbol. In both Eastern and Western religions, a mountain is a symbol of spiritual activity and meditation. The contrast between the golden color of the ocean sunset and the intense blues of the painting determines the color structure of *The Canoe*. In some Russian catalogues and probably in M.A. Morozov's collection, the painting was called *Tahitian Family*.

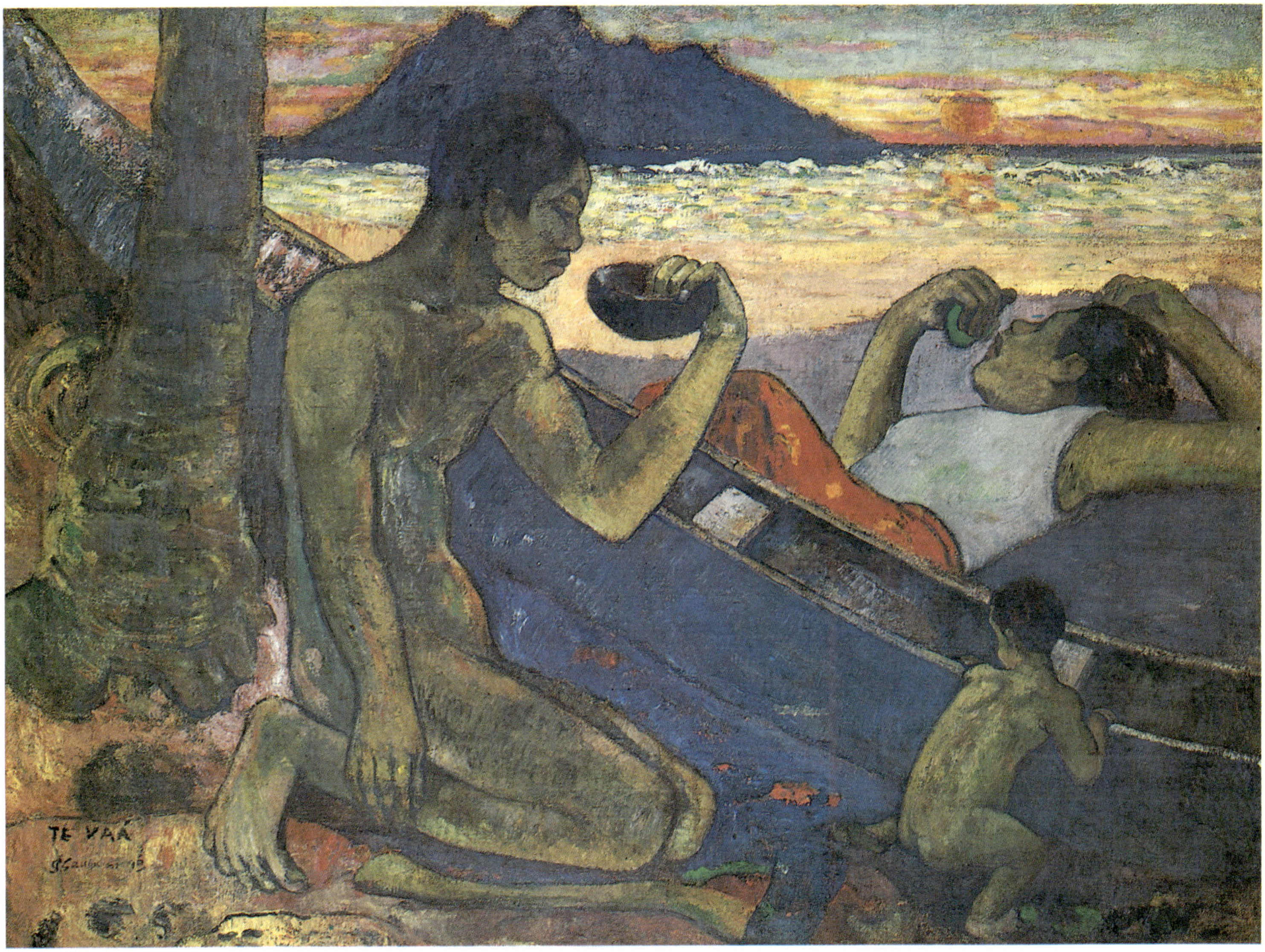
TE VAÁ

Paul Gauguin
1848–1903

23. *Relax (Eiaha Ohipa)*, 1896

Oil on canvas, 65 × 75 cm

Inscribed, signed, and dated, bottom left: Eiaha Ohipa—P. Gauguin 96

Pushkin Museum, inv. no. 3267

Provenance: Gauguin sent the picture to Paris in order to include it in the Brussels Exhibition in 1897 (valued at 600 francs); from 1906, Vollard Gallery, Paris; it was bought by S. Shchukin in the Vollard Gallery or in the Drouot Gallery, Paris; 1918–1923, First Museum of Modern Western Painting, Moscow; 1923–1948, Museum of Modern Western Art, Moscow; since 1948, Pushkin Museum, Moscow.

This work was painted in his studio in Punaauia during Gauguin's second trip to Tahiti. The inscription on the painting has been translated several ways: "Do not do it," meaning do not smoke (Bouge); Danielsson translated the name word-for-word from the Tahitian as "Do not work," since he thought Gauguin wanted to say that the Tahitians did nothing but dream as they considered the dream state to be one of bliss. The lefthand figure was repeated by Gauguin in several versions of the picture *Are You Jealous?* (cat. no. 19), while the poses of the Tahitians were also repeated in the painting *The Gold of Their Bodies*. It may well be that Gauguin borrowed the poses of individual figures from the friezes of the Buddhist temple of Borobudur, of which he had photographs. Cooper thought that the figure with a cigarette in its hands and in a white apron belonged to a man.

A comparison of the enclosed world of an interior with the boundless expanse of nature visible through an open door in the background can be found in another of Gauguin's works, *The Dream*, painted in 1897 in Punaauia. A similar landscape is shown through the door opening in the painting called *Te Faaturuma*, which includes the same dog, shown in profile at the threshold, and the same Tahitian in a hat inside. The name of the latter painting is translated as "Silence" or "Meditation" and refers to the figure of a Tahitian woman shown deep in thought on the floor of her hut. *Te Faaturuma* and *The Dream* help one to understand the meaning of the Moscow picture.

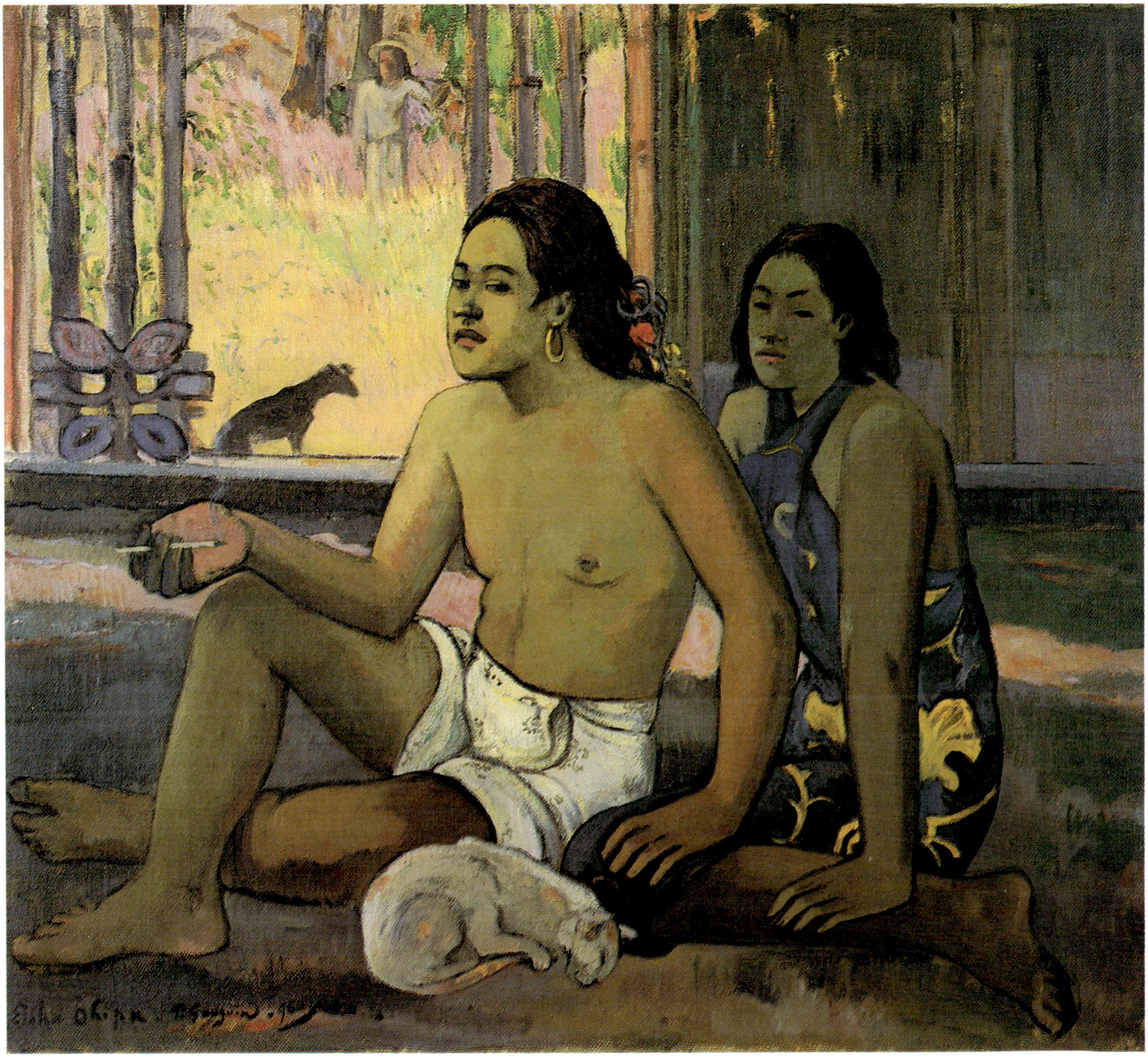

Vincent van Gogh

(Groot-Zundert 1853–
Auvers-sur-Oise 1890)

Van Gogh grew up among strict Calvinists (his father and grandfather were pastors) at Zundert in Brabant (Holland) near the Belgian frontier. He was a normal, sociable youth; mental illness was yet to come. The main trouble was that hardly anyone, except his brother Theo, responded to his passionate exuberance, hence the growing isolation that affected his later life so tragically. After a peripatetic period from 1869 to 1886 of travel, evangelical work in Belgium, sporadic jobs, romantic disillusionment, and confrontations with his tyrannical father, van Gogh seriously took up drawing and painting. Apart from lessons with Auton Mauve in The Hague and at the Academy in Antwerp, where he fell under the spell of Rubens and first purchased Japanese prints, van Gogh was virtually self-taught.

Joining Theo, now director of Goupil's Gallery in Paris (1886), van Gogh was overwhelmed by the Impressionists. Through Theo, who continued to support him financially and morally, he met Pissarro, Degas, Gauguin, and Signac; and at Cormon's studio, where he studied, he became friendly with Toulouse-Lautrec and Emile Bernard. As a result his palette lightened, and he adopted the subject matter and brushwork of the Impressionists. He also experimented with Seurat's pointillist technique.

Van Gogh moved to Arles in February 1888. He continued to make stylistic experiments, trying the "cloisonné" style of the Pont-Aven School, and he drew inspiration from Japanese prints; he also studied artists as different as Giotto, Millet, and Puvis de Chavannes. Rejecting the Impressionists' palette and the Divisionists' Pointillism, van Gogh began using a heavy impasto and intense color, often for symbolic reasons. His subjects, too, involved a private kind of symbolism, as the artist explained in the eloquent letters he wrote to his brother. For the next two years, van Gogh's energy knew no bounds. Thanks largely to him, Fauvism and Expressionism became possible.

Van Gogh's ambition was to establish an artistic commune in his "little yellow house," but only Gauguin took him up on the idea—with disastrous consequences. Although they exerted a mutual influence on one another, they argued incessantly. Following one such drunken row, van Gogh retired to his room and slashed off part of his left ear. After leaving the hospital at Arles, van Gogh recovered only to relapse and have himself committed (May 1889) to the asylum at Saint-Rémy. In May 1890, Theo arranged for his brother to be put in the care of Dr. Gachet, an art collector and amateur painter, at Auvers. Van Gogh's first paintings at Auvers are relatively calm, but his brushwork soon becomes more violent and expressive. On July 27, near the site of the wheat field with crows which he had painted several days earlier, the artist shot himself in the chest, and he died two days later in the presence of the ever-loyal Theo.

Vincent van Gogh
1853–1890

24. *A View of the Arena in Arles,* 1888

Oil on canvas, 73 × 92 cm

Hermitage Museum, inv. no. 6529

Provenance: 1905, Shchukin collection, Moscow; 1918, First Museum of Modern Western Painting, Moscow; 1923, Museum of Modern Western Art, Moscow; since 1931, Hermitage, Leningrad.

This picture was painted in November of 1888. Van Gogh took advice for the composition from Gauguin, who had joined him in Arles not long before. The artist painted this work from memory because at the time the weather was not good enough to work outdoors.

Earlier in April of the same year, van Gogh wrote to his friend Bernard about his visit to a bullfight, where he was most impressed by an enormous and colorful crowd of spectators. He was not as interested in the ancient architectural monuments of Arles. For example, the arena depicted here was constructed before the Christian era and is painted by the artist in a manner that says nothing about its architectural merits.

Van Gogh combined personal feelings and symbols in his work and disguised them with realistic details. According to Bernard, yellow was van Gogh's favorite color. It embodied the sun and the south of France where the artist went in search of bright, sunny colors. Round shapes had an irresistible attraction for the painter and reminded him of the sun. In his mind the yellow arena was easily transformed into the sun.

The interaction between the arena and the back of the yellow head in the foreground carries a meaning that is not purely coloristic. The yellow-headed man in the foreground introduces the spectator into the space of the painting. It is possible that this figure may be another self-portrait. If this is true, then the painting is unique among van Gogh's works. The painter, however, did not insist that this was his self-portrait. He showed the figure from the back and left us with only a hint, although a very important one.

The woman in a green dress is easily identified, in spite of the fragmented manner in which the painter depicted her. She is Madame Genu, who owned a railroad café in Arles. Van Gogh painted her portrait in November (Metropolitan Museum of Art, New York) and later made another version of it (D'Orsay Museum, Paris). Ronald Pickvance noted that the two small figures in the center, a woman in a red dress with a baby and a bearded man, were Postmaster Rollin and his wife, who were close friends of van Gogh. By locating the postmaster and his wife in the center of the composition, van Gogh expresses the idea of family—always important to him.

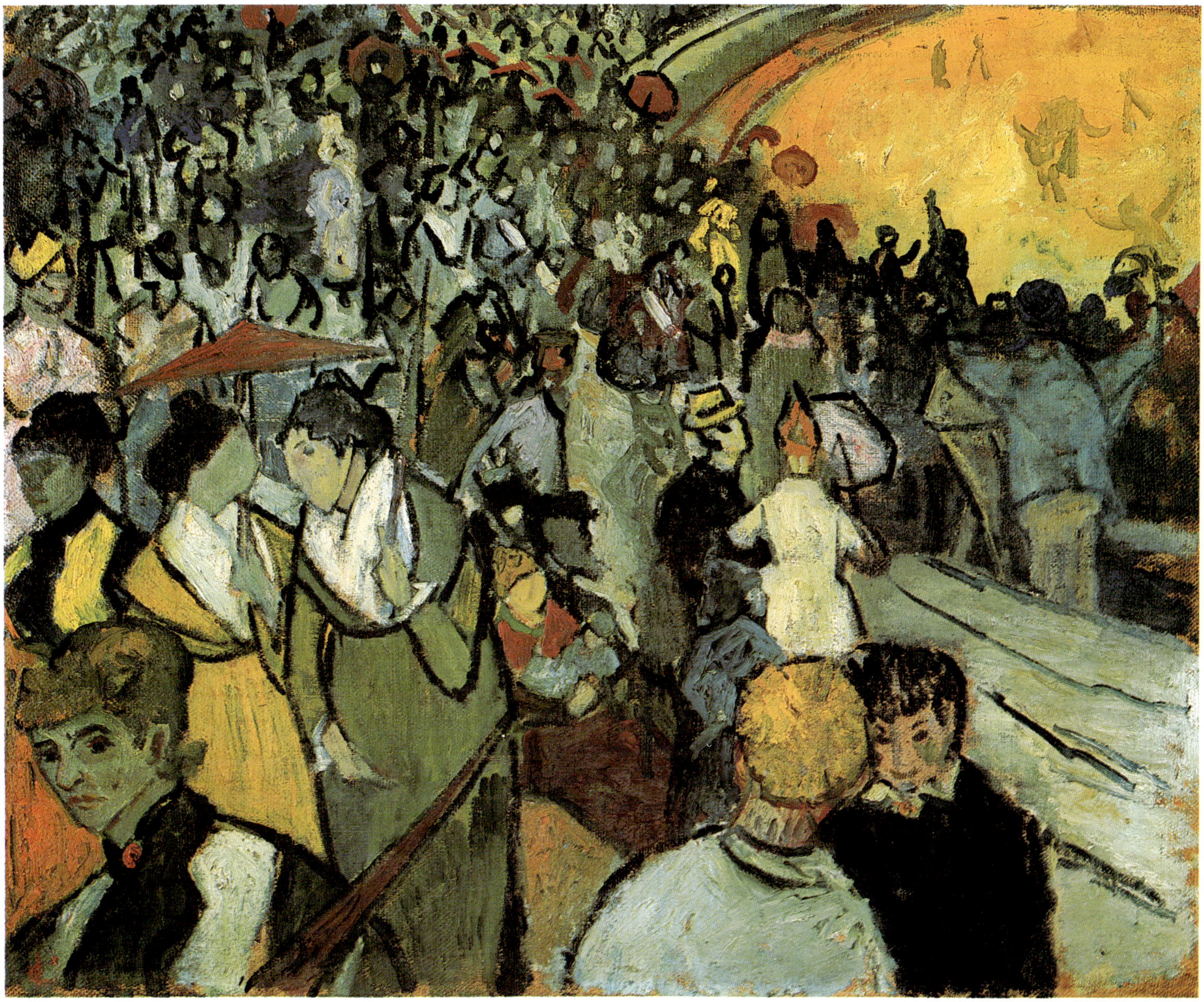

Vincent van Gogh
1853–1890

25. *Portrait of Dr. Félix Rey*, 1889

Oil on canvas, 64 × 53 cm

Signed and dated, bottom right: Vincent Arles 89

Pushkin Museum, inv. no. 3272

Provenance: 1889–1900, Dr. Rey, Arles; 1900, Charles Camoin collection, Paris; 1900, Vollard Gallery, Paris; P. Cassirer Gallery, Berlin, no. 3487; 1908, Druet Gallery, Paris, no. 4285; 1908, Shchukin collection, Moscow; 1918, First Museum of Modern Western Painting, Moscow; 1923, Museum of Modern Western Art, Moscow; since 1948, Pushkin Museum, Moscow.

This portrait depicts Dr. Félix Rey (1865–1932), an intern at the hospital in Arles where van Gogh was confined after his first nervous breakdown. Resuming work, van Gogh painted this portrait and presented it to Dr. Rey, for whom he had the deepest respect. *Portrait of Dr. Félix Rey* contains all the characteristic features of van Gogh's individual style: the impulsive strokes that model the jacket and hair, the vigorous and succulent lines that contour his figure and give it a special expressiveness, and the nervous background decorated by intricate patterns that also serve to bring to life the essence of the sitter's character. Dr. Rey did not appreciate the portrait and considered it the effort of a miserable madman. For a long time, Dr. Rey used the portrait to cover a hole in his chicken house. In 1900, Charles Camoin, who visited places where van Gogh had lived in search of his paintings, found the portrait there.

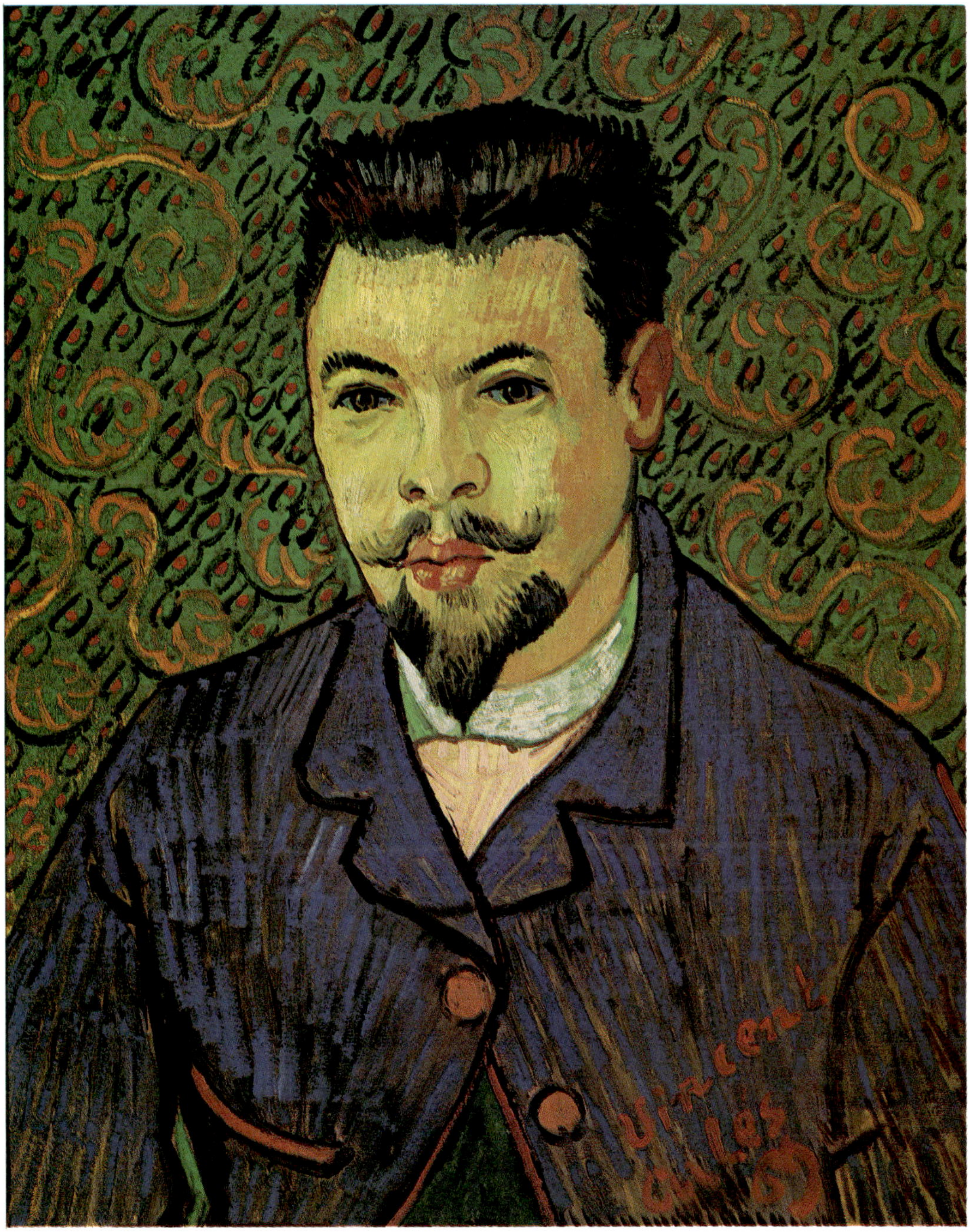
Vincent
Arles

Vincent van Gogh
1853–1890

26. *The Prison Courtyard*, 1890

Oil on canvas, 80 × 64 cm

Pushkin Museum, inv. no. 3373

Provenance: Madame van Gogh-Bönger collection, Amsterdam; Madame Slavona collection, Paris; M. Fabre collection, Paris; 1906, Druet Gallery, Paris, no. 542; 1909, Prince de Wagram collection, Paris; 1909, Druet Gallery, Paris; 1909, I. Morozov collection, Moscow; 1918, Second Museum of Modern Western Painting, Moscow; 1923, Museum of Modern Western Art, Moscow; since 1948, Pushkin Museum, Moscow.

In February 1890, in the asylum at Saint-Rémy, van Gogh made a number of oil copies of well-known paintings and engravings reproduced in the books his brother Theo had sent to him. *The Prison Courtyard* was painted in 1890 from an illustration in an album called *London* and was a free copy of Gustave Doré's drawing engraved by N.J. Pisan (*London, A Pilgrimage by Gustave Doré and Blanchard Jerrold*, London, 1872, p. 136; second issue, Louis Enault, Hachette, Paris, 1876, p. 294).

In a letter to his brother, van Gogh wrote, "This is not a copy, but rather a translation into a different language . . . the language of colors (and) impressions produced by black and white images. . . . I tried to copy Doré's *Exile*—very difficult. . . ." (Letters of Vincent van Gogh to his brother Theo, Paris, 1937, nos. 623 and 626.) While preserving Doré's composition, van Gogh nevertheless put more emphasis upon the expressiveness of the scene. One can recognize the artist depicted in the foreground with a bare head and his hands tucked into his pockets. The stay at the Saint-Rémy asylum reminded van Gogh of Dostoyevsky's *Notes from the House of the Dead*, which he had once read. The image of human despair is convincingly created here by choosing an appropriate color scheme of predominantly earthy grayish-green tones.

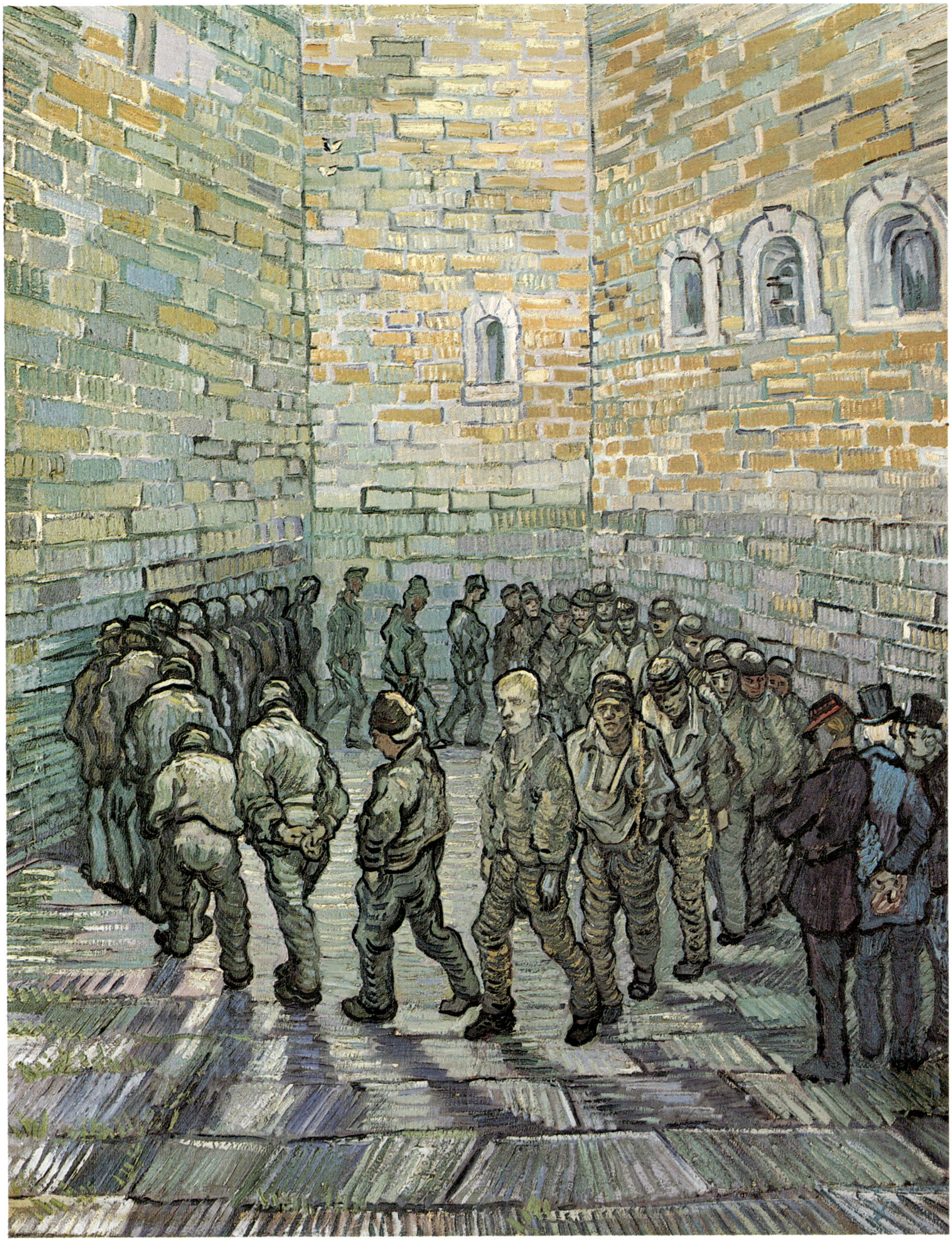

Henri Matisse
1869–1954

27. *Conversation*, 1909

Oil, distemper on canvas, 177 × 217 cm

Hermitage Museum, inv. no. 6521

Provenance: 1912, Shchukin collection, Moscow; 1918, First Museum of Modern Western Painting, Moscow; 1928, Museum of Modern Western Art, Moscow; since 1930, Hermitage, Leningrad.

Painted in Paris in 1909, probably at the end of the summer after the painter had returned from Cavaliero, this picture depicts Matisse and his wife, Emily, although later Matisse remembered that his goal was not to paint a portrait but rather to paint a large composition. *Conversation* is one of the most important works of Matisse's early period and serves as a link connecting two other major pictures of the prewar period: *Red Room* and *Family Portrait*.

In *Conversation* Matisse returns to the problem of the color blue, which bothered him in his *Harmony in Blue*. As a result, it became *Harmony in Red*. The picture is almost the same size as the *Red Room*, but more monumental. Here the details are not as dependent upon ornament, although ornament is included in the composition as the central motif. A black grid links the figures and the background and also serves to join the two themes of the man and the woman together. There were two conflicting beginnings for this painting, which explains why the figures face each other, unlike the composition of any other paintings by Matisse.

In August 1912, when it is believed that Shchukin purchased *Conversation*, he wrote to Matisse: "I think a lot about your blue painting (with two figures). It looks to me like a Byzantine enamel, as rich and as deep in color. This is one of the most wonderful paintings which will remain in my memory."

The traditional dating of the *Conversation* to 1909 seems quite convincing as it was determined by Barr, who had discussed it with the painter himself and his son Pierre.

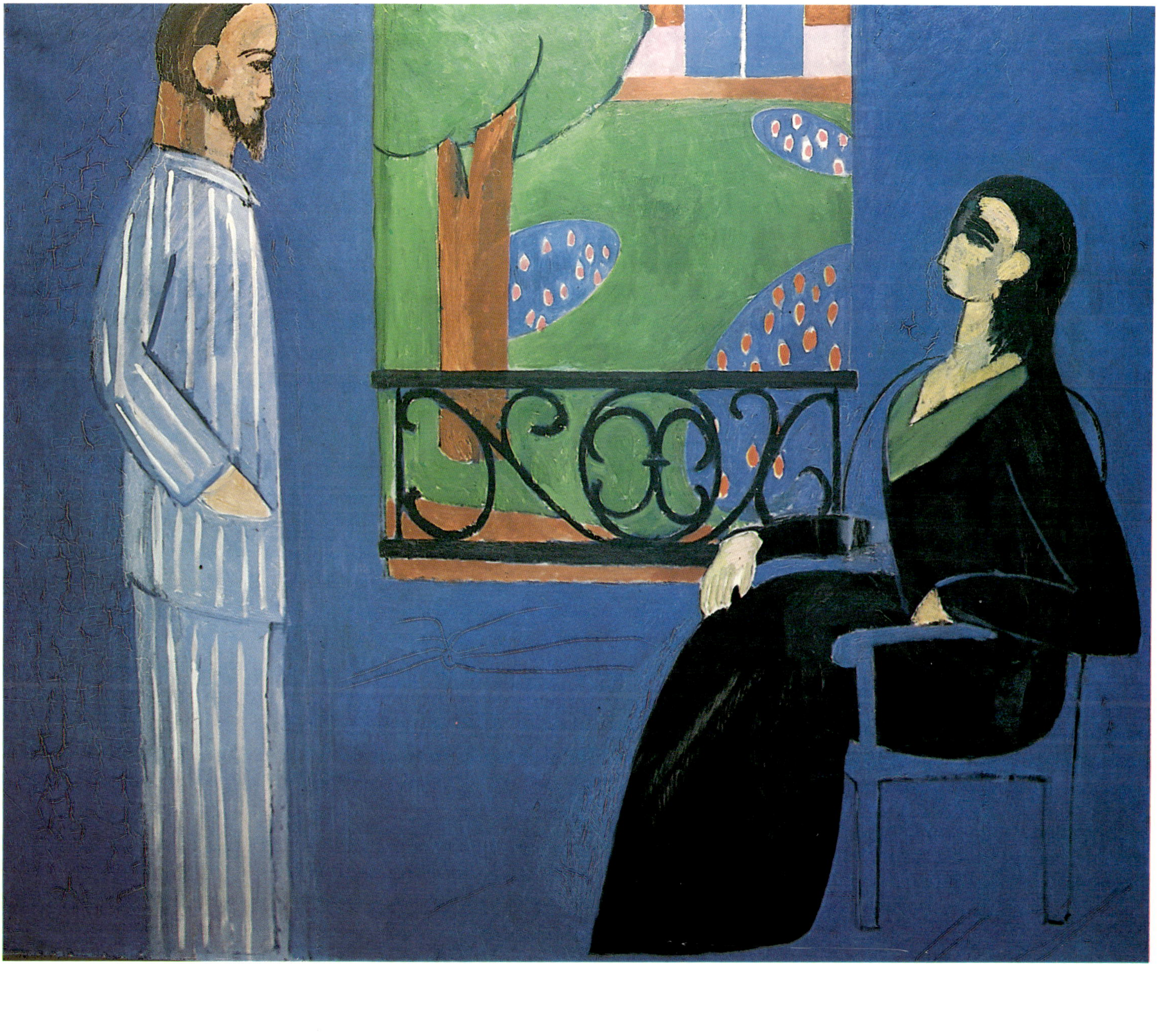

Henri Matisse
1869–1954

28. *Spanish Woman with a Tambourine,* 1909

Oil on canvas, 92 × 73 cm

Signed and dated, bottom left: Henri Matisse, 1909

Pushkin Museum, inv. no. 3297

Provenance: Bernheim-Jeune Gallery, Paris; Shchukin collection, Moscow; 1918, First Museum of Modern Western Painting, Moscow; 1923, Museum of Modern Western Art, Moscow; since 1948, Pushkin Museum, Moscow.

This picture belongs to the period in his career when Matisse was under the strong influence of Fauvism. This is evidenced by the vivid, expressive manner of painting, with contrasting colors and thick black contour lines that create a border between the figure of the Spanish woman and the background. The apparently naïve expressive language of this work calls to mind crudely painted folk sculptures.

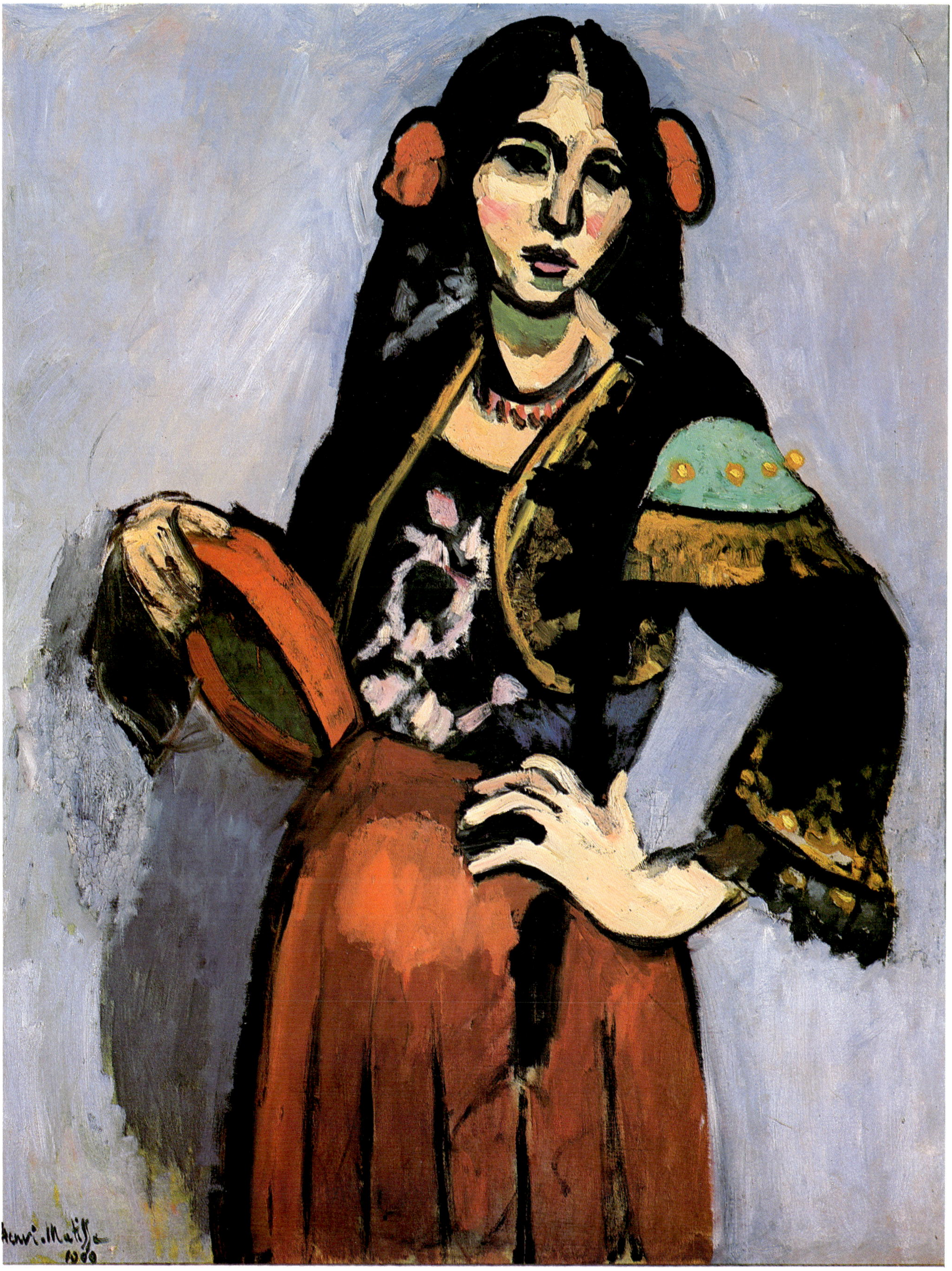

Henri Matisse

1869–1954

29. *Goldfish,*
1911

Oil on canvas, 140 × 98 cm

Pushkin Museum, inv. no. 3299

Provenance: 1912, bought by S. Shchukin from Matisse, Paris; 1912, Shchukin collection, Moscow; 1918, First Museum of Modern Western Painting, Moscow; 1923, Museum of Modern Western Art, Moscow; since 1948, Pushkin Museum, Moscow.

This work was completed in 1911 in the artist's studio at Issy-les-Moulineaux in the suburbs of Paris. Matisse painted the goldfish motif more than a dozen times between 1911 and 1915. In each painting he changed the shape and location of the aquarium and its surroundings. This example is one of the most famous of his variations on the theme. Elderfeld listed six paintings with an aquarium and goldfish, including this one. He attributed to this series *Goldfish* in the Museum of Modern Art, New York (1911); *Goldfish* in the Copenhagen State Art Museum (1912); *Goldfish* from the Barnes collection in Merion, Pennsylvania (1912); *Zorah on the Terrace* (1913, Pushkin Museum); and *Arab Coffeehouse* (1912–1913, Hermitage).

On the basis of S. Shchukin's letter to Matisse of August 22, 1912, in which Shchukin inquires of the painter whether he sent him his paintings from Paris to Moscow, Barr dated the Pushkin Museum picture to 1912; Elderfeld wrote that Madame Doutoue dated the Pushkin Museum painting to 1911. Esholier has called this painting *Bocal de Poissons dans la Serre.*

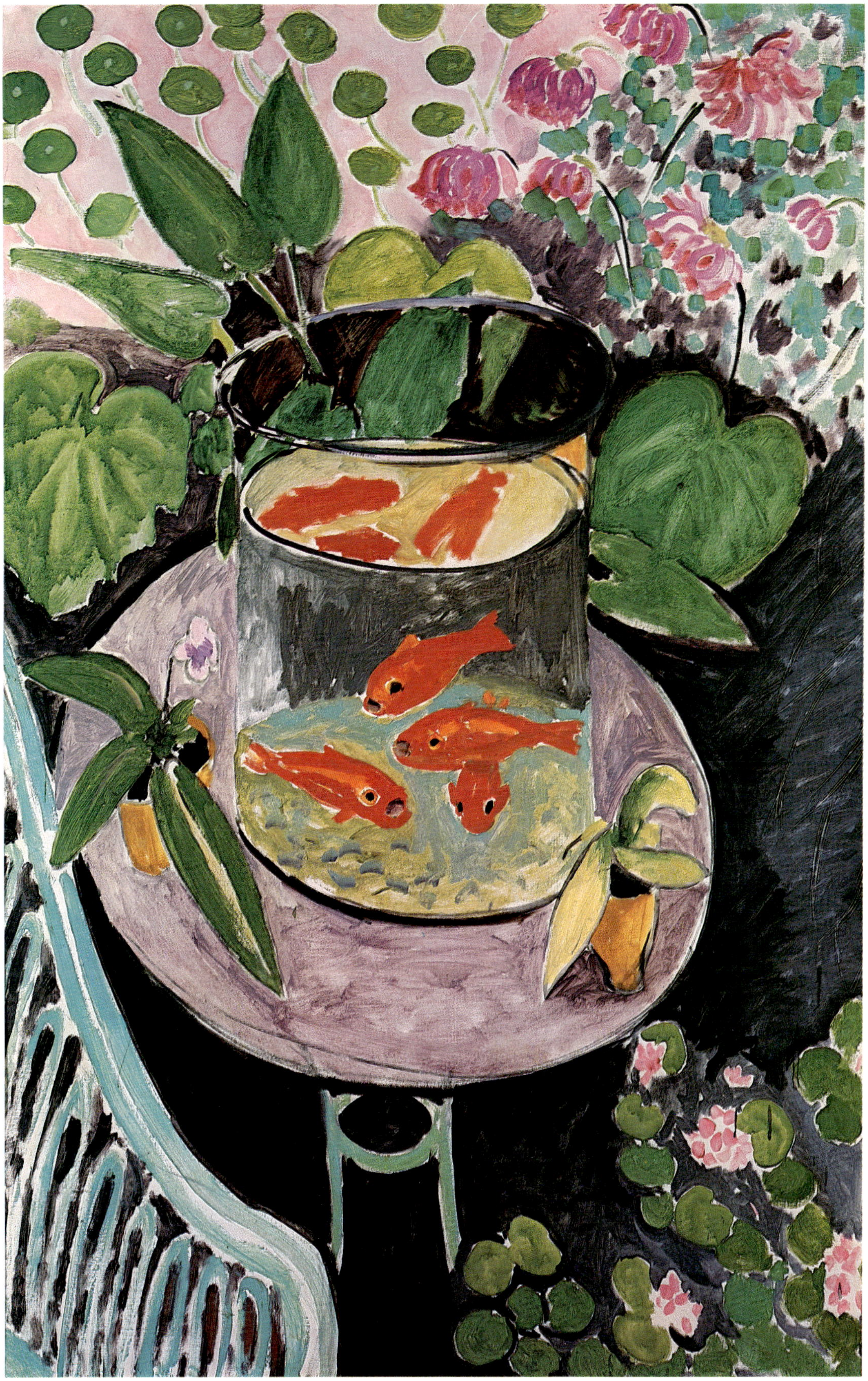

Henri Matisse
1869–1954

30. *Moroccan In Green,*
1911–1913

Oil on canvas, 145 × 96.5 cm

Signed, bottom right: Henri Matisse

Hermitage Museum, inv. no. 9155

Provenance: 1913, Shchukin collection, Moscow; 1918, First Museum of Modern Western Painting, Moscow; 1923, Museum of Modern Western Art, Moscow; since 1948, Hermitage, Leningrad.

There is a label on the back of the canvas that bears an inscription from the painter: *Henri Matisse, Hotel de France, Tanger*, which allows one to conclude that the picture was painted in this hotel at the beginning of 1913.

The painting is also known as *Standing Man of Riff*, as opposed to another painting called *Seated Man of Riff* (Barnes Foundation, Merion, Pennsylvania). Both paintings depict the same Riffian warrior in the same outfit. Agnes Amber, in her references to Gaston Diehl's book (*Henri Matisse*, Paris, 1954, p. 140), states that *Standing Man of Riff* was painted after the much larger picture in the Barnes Foundation, "however, it can easily be a preliminary sketch." Although both paintings are similar in their approach to and handling of color, prominent differences remain. For example, in *Seated Man of Riff* the background is composed of green and yellow lines, and their compositions differ considerably.

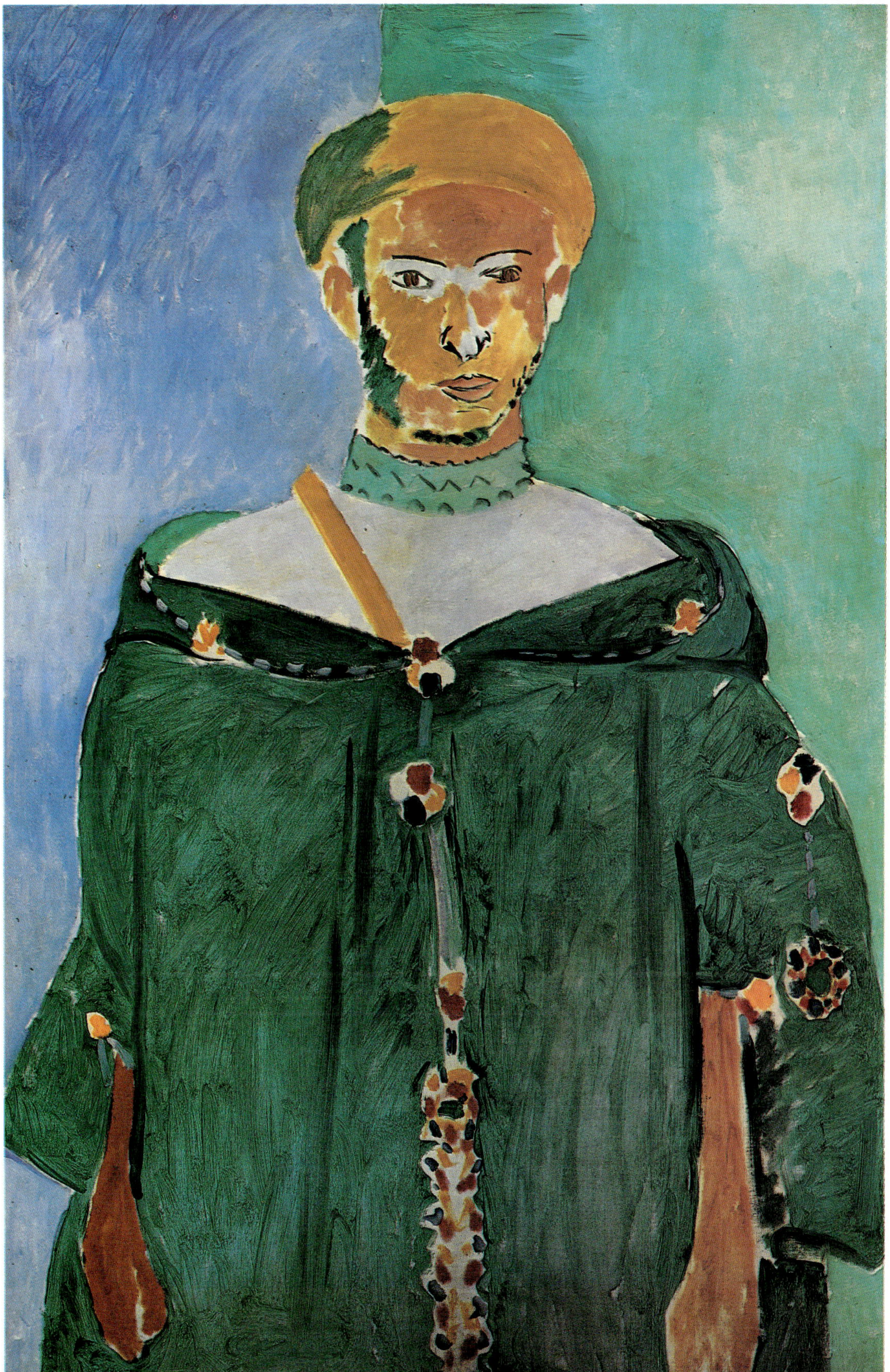

Henri Matisse
1869–1954

31. *Nasturtiums with "La Danse,"* 1912

Oil on canvas, 190.5 × 114 cm

Signed, bottom right: Henri Matisse

Pushkin Museum, inv. no. 3301

Provenance: 1912, S. Shchukin collection, Moscow; 1918, First Museum of Modern Western Painting, Moscow; 1923, Museum of Modern Western Art, Moscow; since 1948, Pushkin Museum, Moscow.

In the summer of 1912, Matisse created this picture at his studio at Issy-les-Moulineaux in the suburbs of Paris. This work is one half of a pair of which the second is called *Corner of the Studio*. This pair of pictures, together with a third "pink" painting called *The Painter's Studio*, form a triptych that decorated S. Shchukin's mansion in Moscow. Shchukin had commissioned Matisse to produce them. All three canvases are now in the Pushkin Museum. From Shchukin's letter to Matisse of August 22, 1912, it is clear that the collector agreed to include *Nasturtiums with "La Danse"* in the Autumn Salon of that year and brought the painting from Moscow to Paris for this purpose. At the same time Matisse painted Shchukin's picture, he also painted another version which now belongs to the Worcester Museum of Art (Massachusetts, USA). This second version differs from the Pushkin Museum painting in its composition. For example, the diagonal line of the floor is straightened and the massive jar with flowers is depicted in a more plastic manner, while in the Pushkin Museum version the jar mingles with the background and the dancing figures look three-dimensional. This play of realistic objects that seem to melt into their background of protruding ornaments gives the Pushkin Museum canvas special sophistication. *Nasturtiums with "La Danse"* depicts a fragment of the painting called *La Danse* (1909, Museum of Modern Art, New York). The dance motif was introduced for the first time by Matisse in his famous picture *La Joie de Vivre* (Barnes Foundation, USA), while another painting titled *La Danse*, a major canvas dedicated to this subject, was also painted on Shchukin's order and is now in the Hermitage Museum, Leningrad.

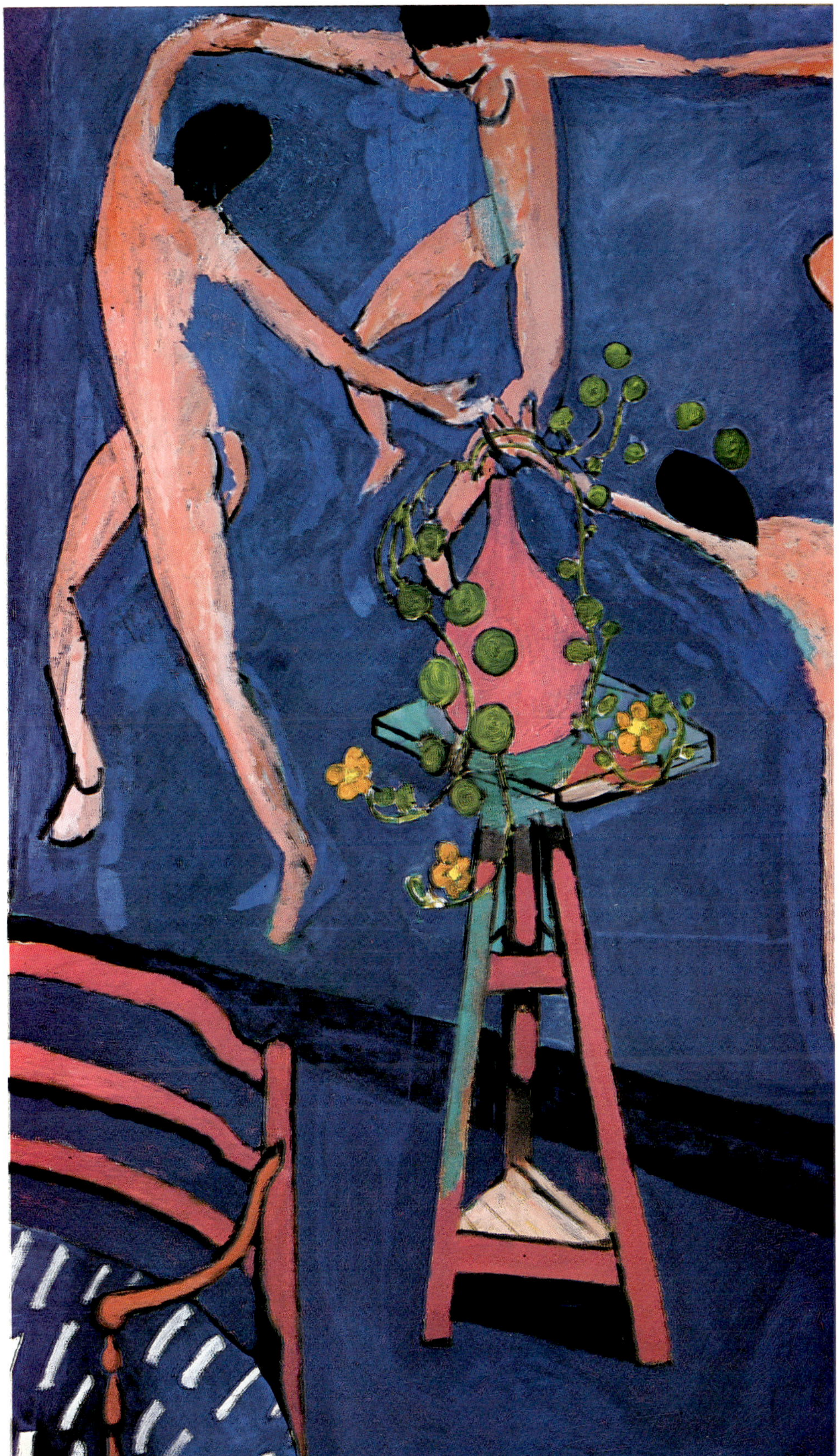

Henri Matisse
1869–1954

32. Bouquet on the Veranda,
1913

Oil on canvas, 146 × 97 cm

Hermitage Museum, inv. no. 7700

Provenance: 1913, Shchukin collection; 1918, First Museum of Modern Western Painting, Moscow; 1923, Museum of Modern Western Art, Moscow; since 1934, Hermitage, Leningrad.

This still life was painted in Tangier, Morocco, at the beginning of 1913. At about the same time, Matisse painted two more still life paintings of the same size: *Open Window in Tangier* (no. 119 of the Matisse Paris Exhibition of 1970) and *Azure Vase with Flowers on a Blue Tablecloth* (Pushkin Museum). The latter painting depicts arum, iris, and lilac. Arum is also represented in the Hermitage still life painted at approximately the same time as the Pushkin Museum picture. One can assume that the present example was painted after the *Azure Vase*, as it was Matisse's usual practice to create a composition and then simplify it in a succession of paintings. Compared to the Pushkin Museum painting, the color of the flowers in the Hermitage canvas was simplified to the point that the painter let sections of the uncovered primed canvas remain in the finished work.

This picture is also known as *Bouquet of Flowers in a Grey Vase on a Veranda* and *Vase with Flowers*.

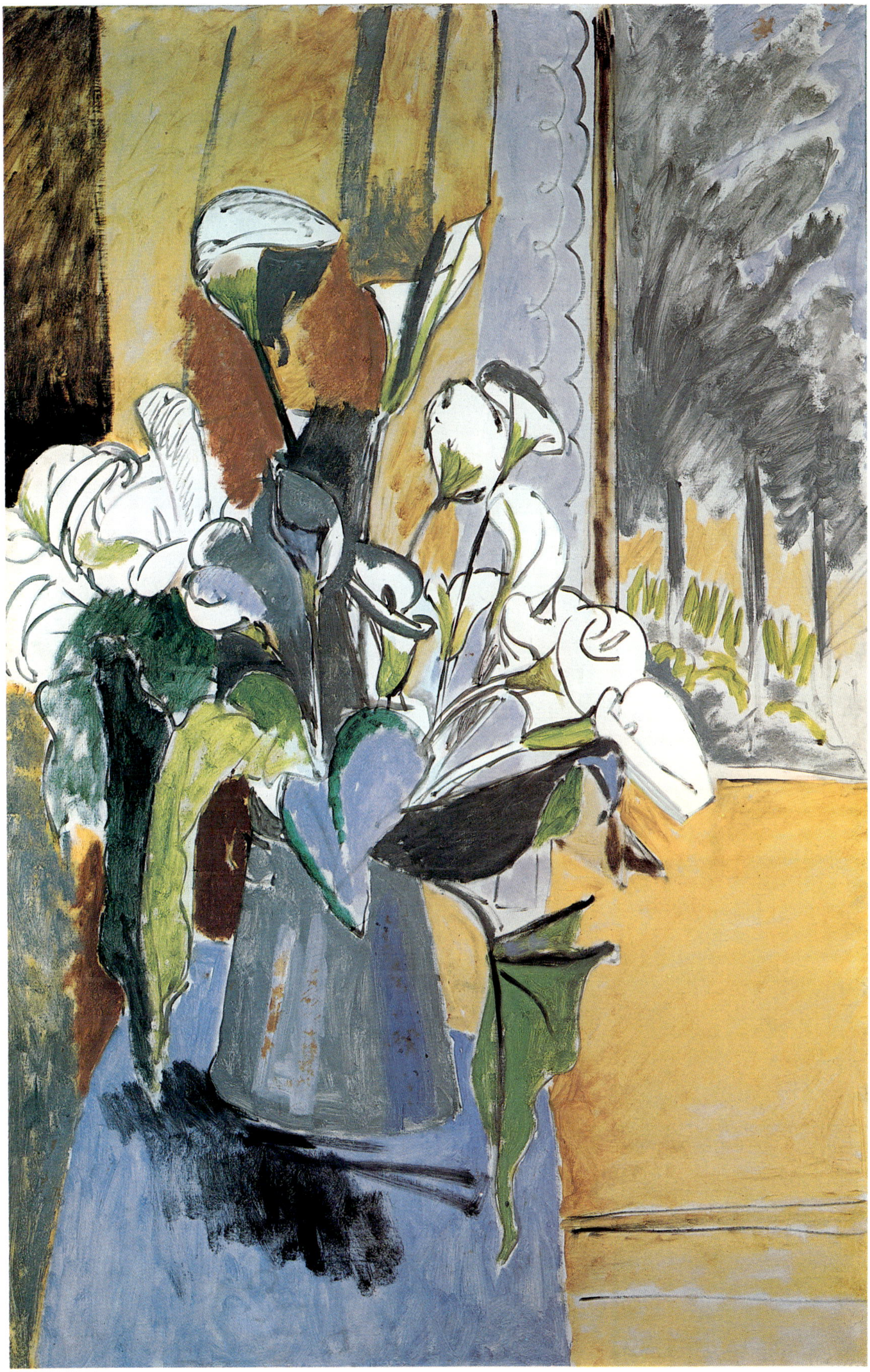

Pablo Ruiz Picasso

(Malaga 1881–Mougins 1973)

A prodigy at thirteen, Picasso spent his formative years in Barcelona, the most progressive and independent city in Spain. Finding Barcelona confining, he set off (1901) for Paris, which became his permanent home. Picasso acquainted himself with the art of Steinlen, Toulouse-Lautrec, van Gogh, Gauguin, the "Nabis," and devoured all he saw in the Louvre. This artistic gorging resulted in a succession of violent oscillations in style and subject (1900–1901).

By 1906, the poverty and misery of "Blue Period" pictures had abated. Blues give way to pink, and Spanish gloom to Parisian sentiment, but Picasso was too much of a rebel to be satisfied for long with the charms of his so-called "Pink Period." Accordingly, he went off to the Pyrenees in the summer of 1906 to forge a tougher, simpler style based on primitive Iberian sculpture. Back in Paris, he worked out his new ideas in a vast figure composition, the *Demoiselles d'Avignon* (1907). Here at last was the synthesis toward which he had been feeling his way. Iberian sculpture, African art, Cézanne and other influences had been fused into a style that was personal, revolutionary, and expressive. A new kind of conceptual, as opposed to perceptual, approach to art was now possible.

In 1907, Picasso met Braque, and for the next seven years the two artists devoted themselves to developing the style known as Cubism. The most influential art movement of the twentieth century, Cubism was never an artistic theory or method, or a magic picture-making formula, but a new pictorial means of representing form and space, and re-creating the reality of things. Cubism was constantly subject to modification, because Picasso and Braque, its two creators, were intuitive, as opposed to scientific, in their approach. All they had to guide them were the pioneer discoveries of Cézanne, and these they soon outstripped. Every other tenet of art they questioned and usually condemned: the notion of a single viewpoint, tonal values, chiaroscuro, and, above all, perspective, which they denounced as an eye-fooling trick. "We wanted to paint not what you *see* but what you know is there," Picasso said.

As a reaction against the way second-rate artists were turning Cubism into a formula, Picasso took to doing from 1915 on highly representational portraits in the style of Ingres; this developed into a neo-classical manner. In 1925, a further *volte-face* occurred, when he turned his back on classicism and adopted a convulsive "metamorphic" manner which owes something to Surrealism. The outbreak of civil war in Spain in 1936, apart from inspiring *Guernica*—one of the artist's most powerful pictures—confirmed Picasso in his left-wing allegiances, and these played a key role in his postwar development.

The last years of Picasso's long life were a desperate race against time. The most protean and prolific artist in history was out to pit his work against the greatest masters of the past—Cranach, Velázquez, Rembrandt, Delacroix, Manet, to name but a few. He died building a pantheon around himself.

Pablo Picasso
1881–1973

33. *Harlequin and His Companion*, 1901

Oil on canvas, 73 × 60 cm

Signed, top left: Picasso

Pushkin Museum, inv. no. 3400

Provenance: Bought by I. Morozov from A. Vollard, Paris, 1908, for 300 francs; 1919–1923, Second Museum of Modern Western Painting, Moscow; 1923–1948, Museum of Modern Western Art, Moscow; since 1948, Pushkin Museum, Moscow.

This picture was painted in Paris in the early autumn of 1901 and dedicated to a "modern" scene depicting the life of an artist symbolically as a harlequin. Such a theme is typical for Picasso during his second stay in the French capital. Harlequin, a prominent hero of the "Commedia dell'Arte," is also shown in a picture called *Reclining Harlequin* (Zervos, I.79), painted at about the same time as the present picture, while a related female portrait is shown in a picture called *Woman With a Chignon* (Z.I.96). The abovementioned paintings are stylistically close to *The Absinthe Drinker* from the Hermitage (Z.I.98) and to *Portrait of the Poet Sabartes* in the Pushkin Museum.

The following sketches may be considered preliminary studies for the present work: a pen study of a harlequin figure (Z.XXI.295), a pencil drawing of his female companion (Z.XXI.296), and a drawing depicting a harlequin embracing a woman (Z.XXI.297).

Relating the image of the harlequin to the artist (the painter himself) is confirmed by a later painting of 1905, when Picasso returned to this theme in *At the Lapin Agile* (Z.I.275). In this picture, the painter depicted himself in a harlequin's costume accompanied by a prostitute. Here again, he shows in the foreground the large and small glasses present in the Pushkin Museum canvas, although they serve a different purpose. In the Pushkin Museum painting, the harlequin has the white face of a tragic Pierrot, while his girl friend's face is reminiscent of a Japanese mask. Some scholars have found that the early images of Italian comedy depicted by Picasso are similar to the symbolic images of Verlaine's late poetry (P. Johnson, "Picasso's Parisian Family and the 'Saltimbanques,'" *Arts Magazine*, 51, Jan. 1977, pp. 90–95). A. Podoxic suggests that the images depicted in the painting were taken from Parisian cafés where young actors performed.

The Pushkin Museum painting can be considered one of the best samples of Picasso's "stained-glass panel" period, which was at its best at the end of his second stay in Paris. In the pictures of this period, strong, flexible, and dark contours separating figures and objects from their realistic surroundings play the major role in creating separate, lonely images. *Harlequin and His Companion* is painted over another unknown earlier picture. Painting over a previously made or even a freshly painted picture became characteristic of Picasso's work at the end of 1901, which marked the beginning of a new stylistic period that was later called his "Blue Period."

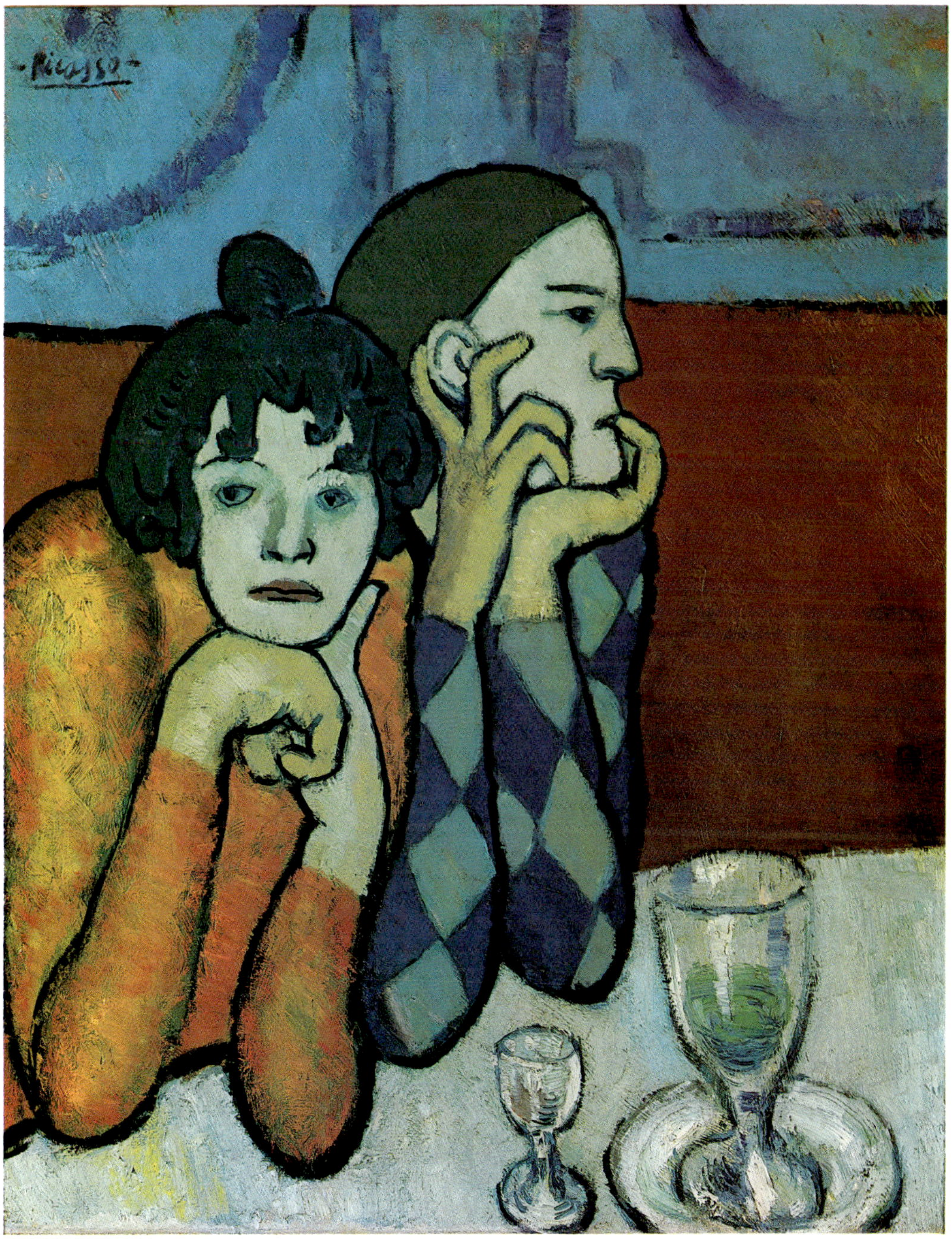
Picasso

Pablo Picasso
1881–1973

34. *Portrait of the Tailor José Maria Soler*, 1903

Oil on canvas, 100 × 70 cm

Signed and dated, top left: Picasso 1903

Hermitage Museum, inv. no. 6528

Provenance: Soler collection, Barcelona; Kahnweiler Gallery, Paris; Shchukin collection; 1918, First Museum of Modern Western Painting, Moscow; 1923, Museum of Modern Western Art, Moscow; since 1930, Hermitage, Leningrad.

This portrait was painted in Barcelona in the summer of 1903 as part of a trio of works, including *Portrait of Madame Soler* (Neue Pinakothek, Munich) and a large *Portrait of the Soler Family* (Museum of Fine Arts, Liège), in which the head of the family is positioned differently. A pen drawing also exists from the same period showing Soler in a riding habit (Heinz collection, Pittsburgh, Z.XXII.40).

José Maria Soler was a fashionable Barcelona tailor to and friend of Picasso. The painter usually paid for his friend's services with his pictures, and his association with Soler lasted for several years. Max Jacob emphasized that even when Picasso was extremely poor, he took good care of his appearance. In 1899, Picasso made a charcoal profile portrait of Soler (Z.XXI.113), and in 1901 *Arte Joven* printed an illustration: Soler's full figure portrait (Z.VI.310).

The Soler family may not have been satisfied with Picasso's portraits of 1903. Several years later they were all sold.

Pablo Picasso
1881–1973

35. *Woman from Mallorca*, 1905

Tempera and watercolor on cardboard, 67 × 51 cm

Signed, bottom left: Picasso

Pushkin Museum, inv. no. 3316

Provenance: Bought by S. Shchukin in Paris before 1913; 1918–1923, First Museum of Modern Painting, Moscow; 1923–1948, Museum of Modern Western Art, Moscow; since 1948, Pushkin Museum, Moscow.

This picture is the only existing study for the figure of the woman at the extreme right in Picasso's famous canvas *Family of Saltimbanques* (Z.I.285), which belongs to the National Gallery in Washington, D.C. It was probably painted at the end of the summer of 1905 after Picasso returned from Holland. The fact that the model represents the people of Mallorca is confirmed by the characteristic detail of her national costume, the *rebozillo*, or white kerchief.

Palau i Fabre believes that Picasso referred to a woman from a "forgotten island" because he remembered religious holiday processions in Barcelona and also because of the cards and letters he received from his fellow Spaniard and friend, artist Junyer Vidal, who went to Mallorca to paint in the summer of 1905. The special expression on the face of the woman in this work and the overall intriguing aura of the painting are also present in the Mallorca woman of the Washington canvas. The role of the woman's image in the Washington painting remains unclear, and in the preliminary study for the Washington painting, which is also in the Pushkin Museum collection, the female figure is missing.

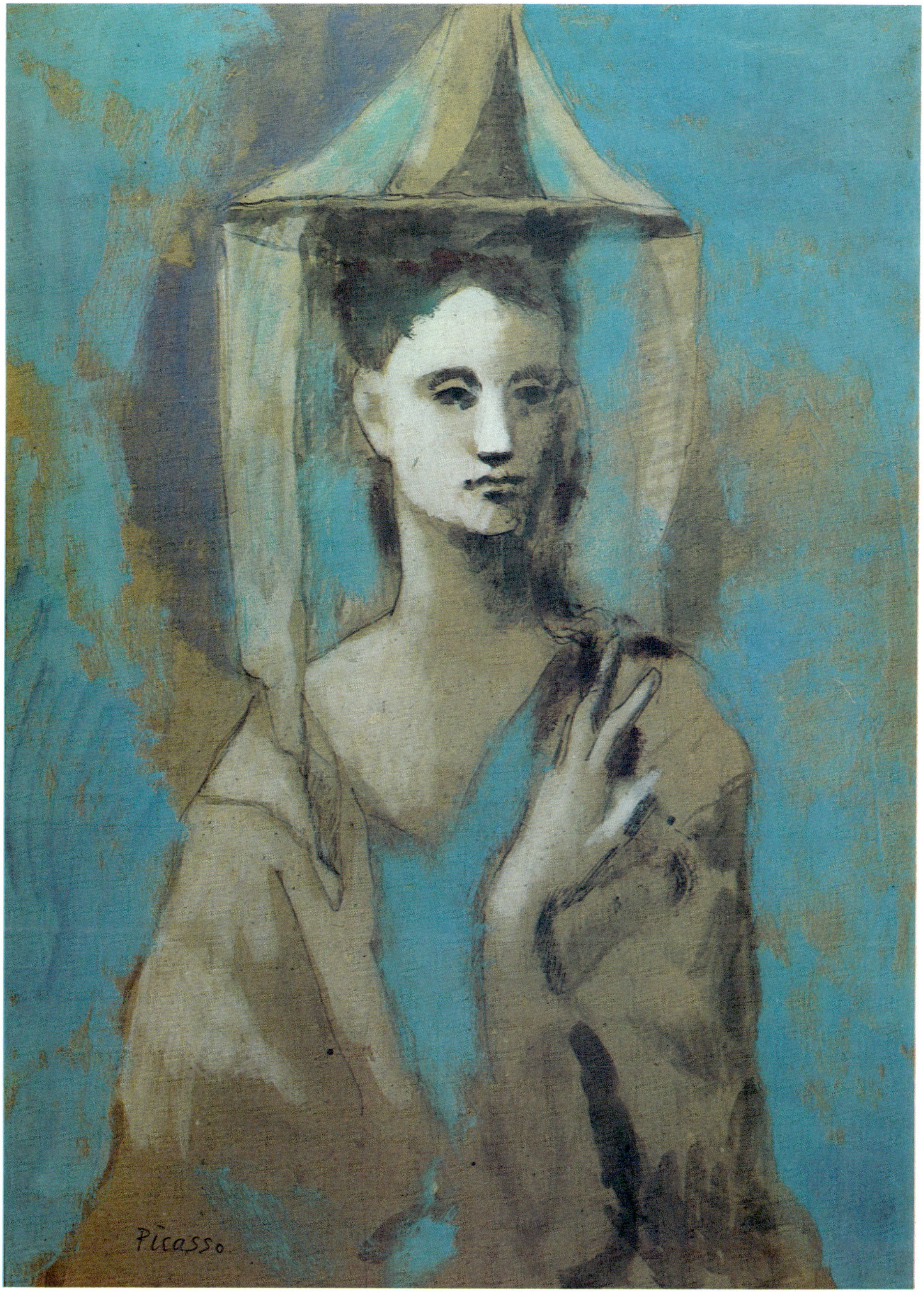
Picasso

Pablo Picasso
1881–1973

36. *Still Life with Skull*, 1907

Oil on canvas, 116 × 89 cm

Signed on the back: Picasso

Hermitage Museum, inv. no. 9162

Provenance: Kahnweiler Gallery, Paris; 1912, Shchukin collection, Moscow; 1918, First Museum of Modern Western Painting, Moscow; 1923, Museum of Modern Western Art, Moscow; since 1948, Hermitage, Leningrad.

This composition reminds us of still life paintings of the "vanitas" type. The choice of objects is dictated by traditional symbolism, and the palette reminds the viewer of the subject's predecessors and indirectly of a slogan popular at the beginning of the 20th century: "ars longa, vita brevis est." The books in the composition represent knowledge, and the pipe symbolizes the pleasures of life. At the same time, all of the images are directed toward the skull, a symbol of death and frailty.

Still Life with Skull occupies a very special place among the works of the Cubists, and it does not seem to belong to any of the groups of early Picasso paintings. The traditional date of 1907 for this painting has recently been questioned. The formal composition of the painting prompts a reference to Picasso's other works of 1907 and 1908. The upper left of the painting reminds us stylistically of his other still life paintings from the summer of 1907; however, the principal lower portion of the canvas is somewhat closer to the paintings from the first half of 1908.

The color of the Hermitage canvas is unusual, as it does not match the approach to the colors of any other of his paintings. This phenomenon has been explained earlier as a reflection of Matisse's influence. More convincing is an explanation given by Theodore Reff, who connects the theme of *Still Life with Skull* with the suicide of the German painter Vigels, who lived near Picasso. Fernande Olivier recalled that at the time it was quite a blow for Picasso. The painter himself said that while working on a painting on June 1, 1908, depicting a nude (Jacqueline Picasso collection, Mouguin, Z.IIXX.694), he suddenly saw Vigels, who had hanged himself in the window of his studio. Picasso made a sketch for *Still Life with Skull* probably in June 1908, soon after Vigels's funeral (Pushkin Museum, Moscow, Z.IIX.49). The present picture was painted soon thereafter.

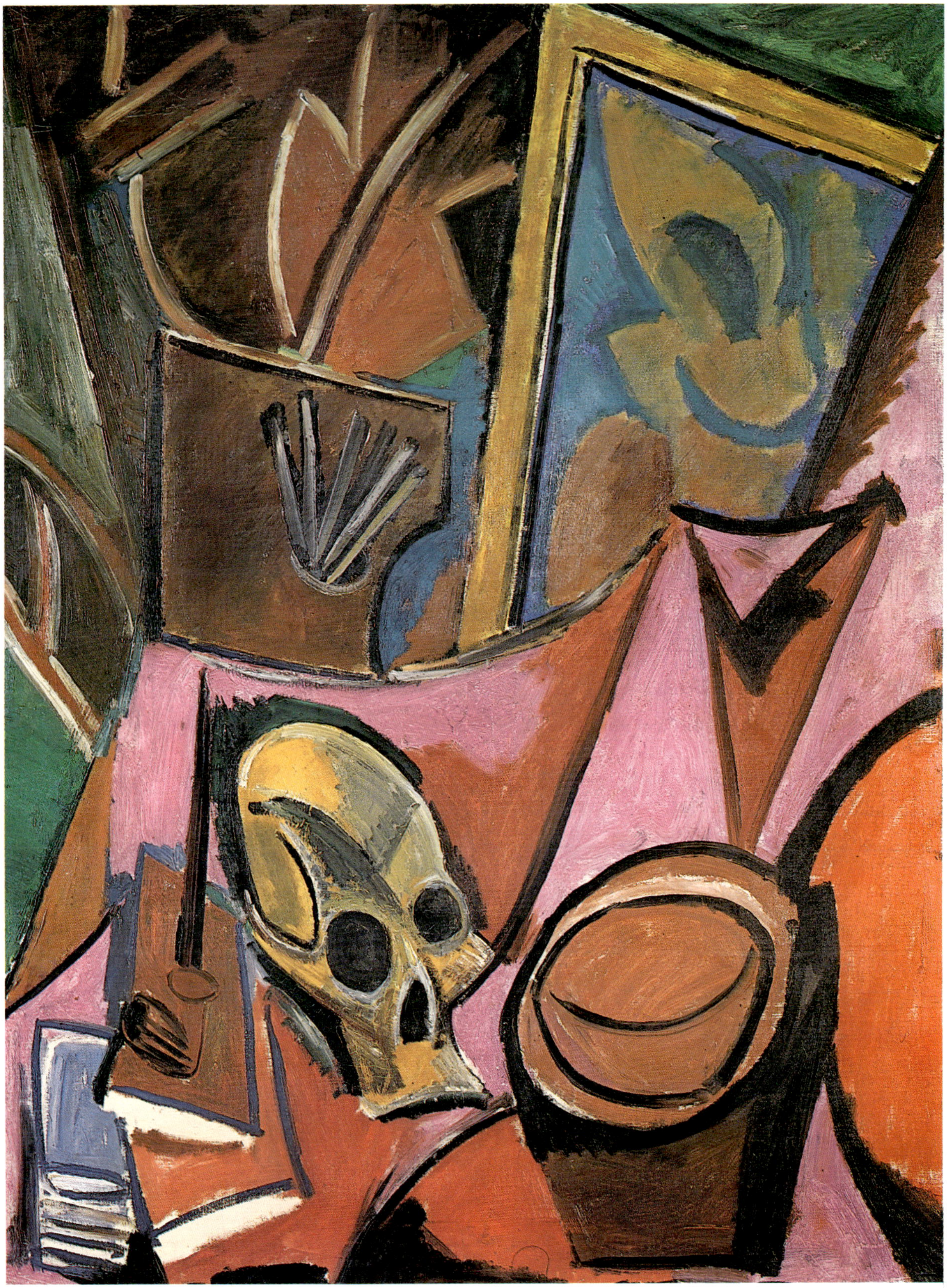

Pablo Picasso
1881–1973

37. *House and Trees,* 1908

Oil on canvas, 92 × 73 cm

Pushkin Museum, inv. no. 3350

Provenance: Bought by S. Shchukin in Paris before 1913; 1918, First Museum of Modern Western Painting, Moscow; 1923, Museum of Modern Western Art, Moscow; since 1948, Pushkin Museum, Moscow.

The Pushkin Museum landscape is traditionally dated August 1908, although A. Podoxic dates the work to the beginning of 1909 and refers it to the so-called Green Period (according to a definition given by G. Stein). As proof, he refers to the similarities between this work and the background in the drawing (Z.XXVI.374) and in the gouache (Z.XXVI.381). Houses of a similar structure can also be found in compositions depicting Hort de Abro, made in the summer of 1909, although in the landscape *Small House and Trees* in the Hermitage collection (Z.II.¹80), made in *La Rue des Bois* in August 1908, both the small house and the trees are interpreted differently than in the Pushkin Museum landscape.

In spite of the tendency of the artist to generalize shapes in the two latter works, they remain close to nature and static, while the Pushkin Museum landscape consists of shapes piled on top of each other, forming a complicated living crystal. Daix correctly called this composition the "intellectual architecture of the canvas" (Daix-Rosselet, p. 52). The deformed parallels of the small house are somewhat close to houses in Braque's landscapes, painted in Estaque in the summer of 1908. One can suggest that Picasso returned to depicting a small house among trees when he lived in Paris and after he saw the landscapes of Braque exhibited at the Kahnweiler Gallery in 1908. The play of three-dimensional shapes on the surface of this canvas and the use of "inverted" perspective in the small house and in the fence of *House and Trees* are characteristic of Picasso's work during the winter and summer of 1909. The dry tree at the left edge of the painting is composed of the same elements used in the nudes painted in the winter of 1909 (*A Bathing Woman,* Z.II.¹III) and suggests a later date for this work.

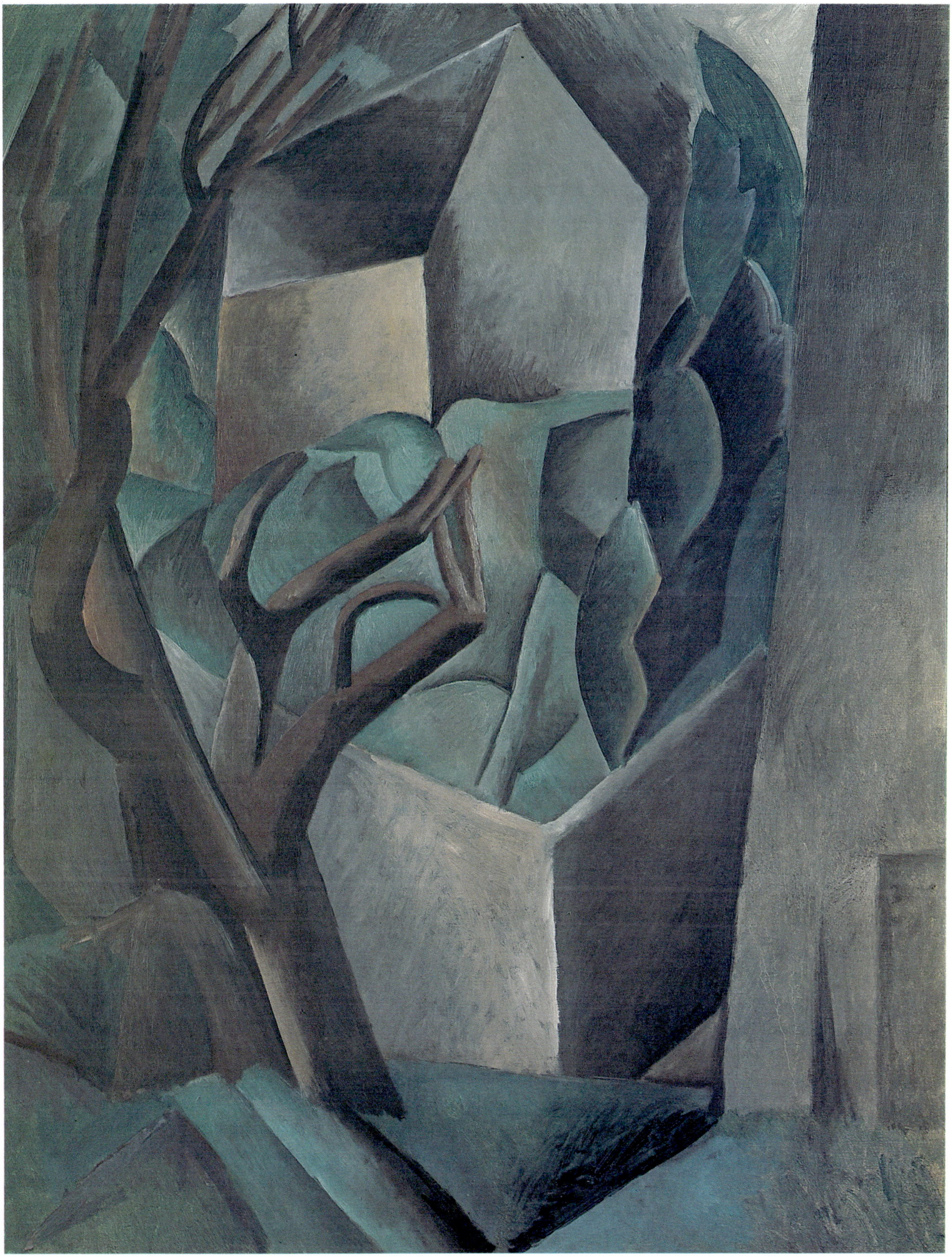

Pablo Picasso
1881–1973

38. *Seated Woman Holding a Fan,* 1908

Oil on canvas, 150 × 100 cm

Hermitage Museum, inv. no. 7705

Provenance: Probably Vollard Gallery in Paris; Shchukin collection; 1918, First Museum of Modern Western Painting, Moscow; 1928, Museum of Modern Western Art, Moscow; since 1934, Hermitage, Leningrad.

This is one of the most important examples of Picasso's early Cubism and was painted in Paris in all likelihood in the autumn of 1908 after Picasso returned from La Rue des Bois.

While in the Shchukin collection, this painting was called *After the Ball.* It is difficult to say whether this name was given to the picture by the painter, as it was not customary for Picasso to give his pictures names of this kind. The name hints at the existence of a theme, probably of a literary type, which was customary for Salon paintings of the time. In 1904, Picasso made a pen sketch called *Away from the Ball* (Z.XXII.86) in which he depicted a seducer sporting a mustache and a sentimental lady holding a fan. However curious the sketch may be, the picture was not a satire. Picasso depicted his hero geometrically and in a monumental scale, colored grotesquely. The pen sketch for the present painting, now kept in the Picasso collection, does not have prominent geometrical forms, and Zervos shows a similar sketch in his catalogue of Picasso's works (Z.II.702). Another sketch (Z.II.701) was made later, probably during Picasso's work on the painting that defines the gesture of the figure more accurately.

An X-ray of this painting has revealed that the woman's head was painted over several times. Close examination of the X-ray reveals that, at first, the woman's eyes were wide open, which had the effect of giving the painting more psychological content. This first version is connected with a sketch of Fernande Olivier mentioned in Zervos's catalogue (Z.II.700).

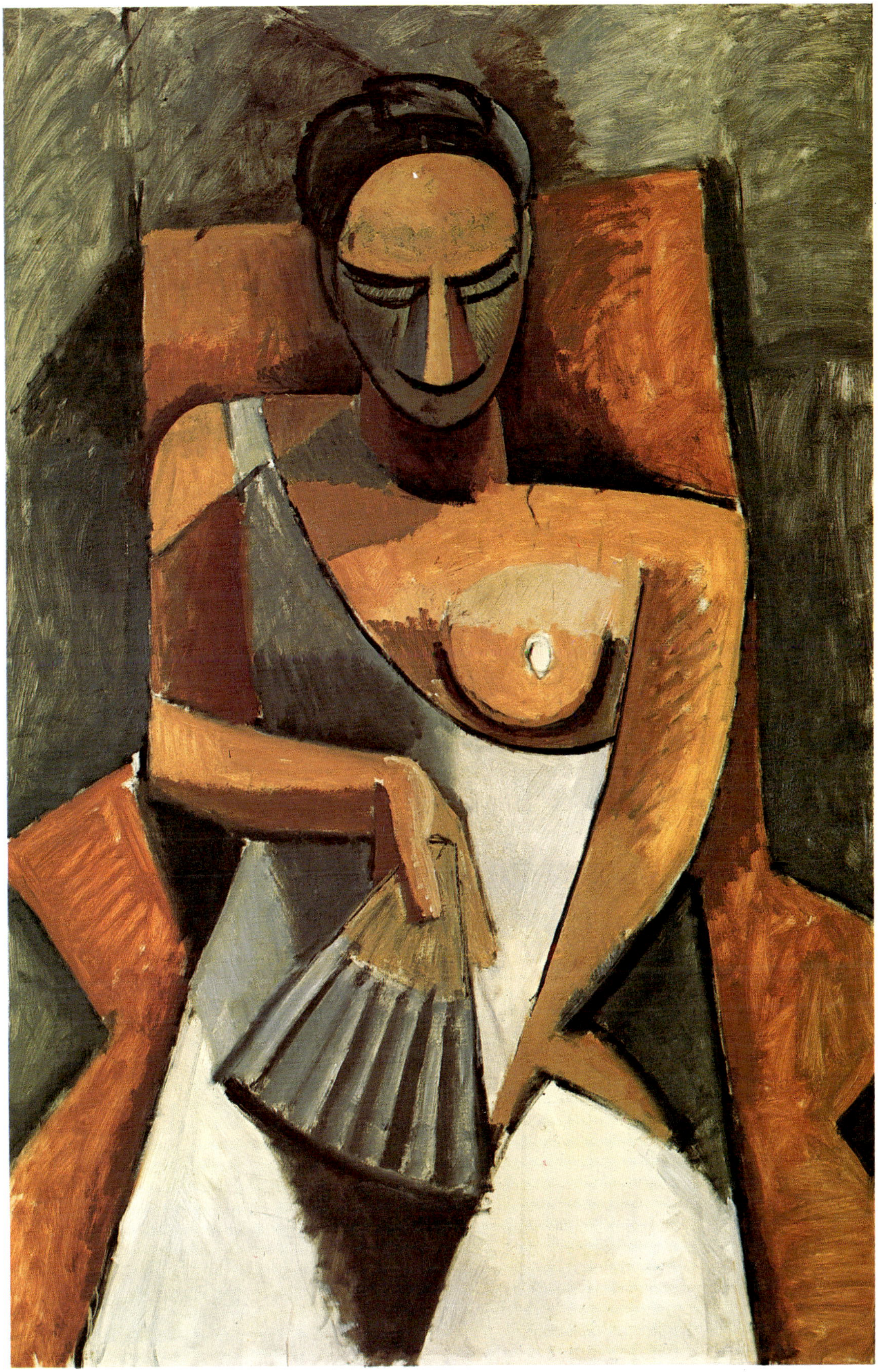

Pablo Picasso
1881–1973

39. *Three Women*, 1908

Oil on canvas, 200 × 178 cm

Prior to recanvasing, the reverse of this painting was signed: Picasso

Hermitage Museum, inv. no. 9658

Provenance: Gertrude Stein collection, Paris (before 1913); 1913, Kahnweiler Gallery, Paris; 1913 or 1914, Shchukin collection, Moscow; 1918, First Museum of Modern Western Painting, Moscow; 1923, Museum of Modern Western Art, Moscow; since 1948, Hermitage, Leningrad.

One of the most important paintings created by Picasso, *Three Women* concluded a period that had started with *Demoiselles d'Avignon* and occupied the artist during all of 1908. About 70 sketches having a direct relationship to this painting are known. The starting point was probably Cézanne's painting *Bathers*, which was presented at the exhibition of the Autumn Salon in 1907 (Kunstmuseum, Basel). Picasso started the work by depicting five figures (Cézanne's work also showed five female nudes). This compositional approach is shown in a watercolor that now belongs to the Museum of Modern Art in New York, *Bathers in a Forest*, which was painted before the Hermitage picture was finished. The upraised arms in the poses of the women indicate that they are washing their backs. In the course of his work on this painting, Picasso changed the number of figures in the composition as well as their poses. The difference between the sketches for this work and the completed painting can be explained by the fact that, in the course of the painting, the Hermitage canvas was changed considerably. In the final version, we see the Three Graces depicted in a revolutionary, modern style. Picasso's connection with classical art is not limited to this scene of Three Graces.

The end of 1908 was a turning point in Picasso's art, and it appears to have happened during his work on *Three Women*. After consultations with the painter, Zervos dated this painting to the last months of 1908. Rubin calls *Three Women* the most important painting of 1908, and one of the key Picasso paintings in the artist's oeuvre. Picasso's sketches for this work reflect African influences and contrasting colors, while in the completed painting he uses more subtle tones. Rubin has explained the lack of African features in this work by suggesting that Picasso had a renewed interest in Cézanne and in Cubism. Steinberg, on the other hand, offers that Picasso was struggling against Cézanne's influence rather than accepting it.

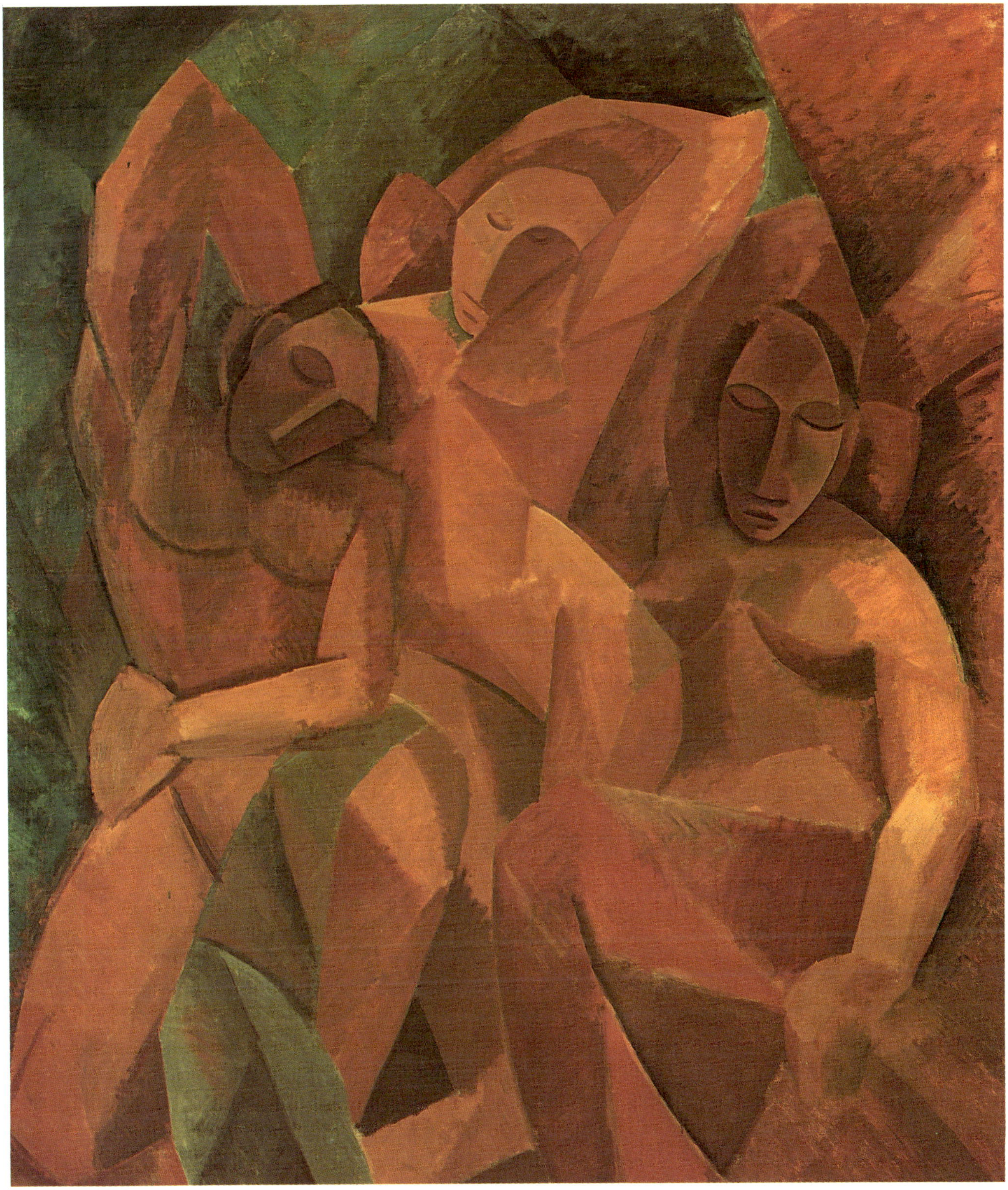

Pablo Picasso
1881–1973

40. *Portrait of Ambroise Vollard,* 1909–1910

Oil on canvas, 93 × 66 cm

Pushkin Museum, inv. no. 3401

Provenance: Bought by I. Morozov from Vollard Gallery, Paris, 1913, for 300 francs; 1918, Second Museum of Modern Western Painting, Moscow; 1923, Modern Museum of Western Art, Moscow; since 1948, Pushkin Museum, Moscow.

Ambroise Vollard (1865–1939) was a prominent Parisian art dealer, connoisseur, and collector of art who also wrote memoirs about Renoir, Cézanne, and Degas. Vollard played a significant role in Picasso's life. He was the first art dealer to notice the young Spanish painter in Paris, and arranged a show for him on June 24, 1901, in his gallery on the Rue Lafitte. He remained in close contact with Picasso until the day he died. In 1927, Vollard commissioned Picasso to make illustrations for Balzac's *Unknown Masterpiece,* and between 1930 and 1937, Vollard purchased the majority of the copper plates of Picasso's etchings. Prints made from these plates are known as the Vollard Suite series. In 1937, Picasso added to this series several portraits of Vollard, and, in addition, there is a pencil drawing by Picasso from 1915 that depicts Vollard in a realistic manner seated in a chair. Yet, the present picture, *Portrait of Ambroise Vollard,* from the Pushkin collection, is the most recognized of the artist's works representing the dealer. Picasso started this portrait at the end of 1909 and finished it in the summer of 1910, which is clear from a letter written by Fernande Olivier to Gertrude Stein on June 17, 1910 (*Picasso Anthology, Criticism, Documents, Reminiscences,* London, 1981, p. 67).

This is the earliest of the three known portraits of Parisian dealers—friends of Picasso, painted in a Cubist manner. The other two are *Portrait de Wilhelm Uhde* (1910, Z.II¹, 217) and *Portrait de Daniel-Henry Kahnweiler* (autumn 1910, Z.II¹, 227). Contemporaries mentioned that there was an amazing similarity between the portrait and the sitter. However, Vollard was not fond of this portrait, even though he considered it an important piece of art, and in 1913 he sold it to I. Morozov. It is known that Morozov, unlike Shchukin, did not really like Cubism. Perhaps he was attracted by the portrait's expressiveness and by the sitter himself.

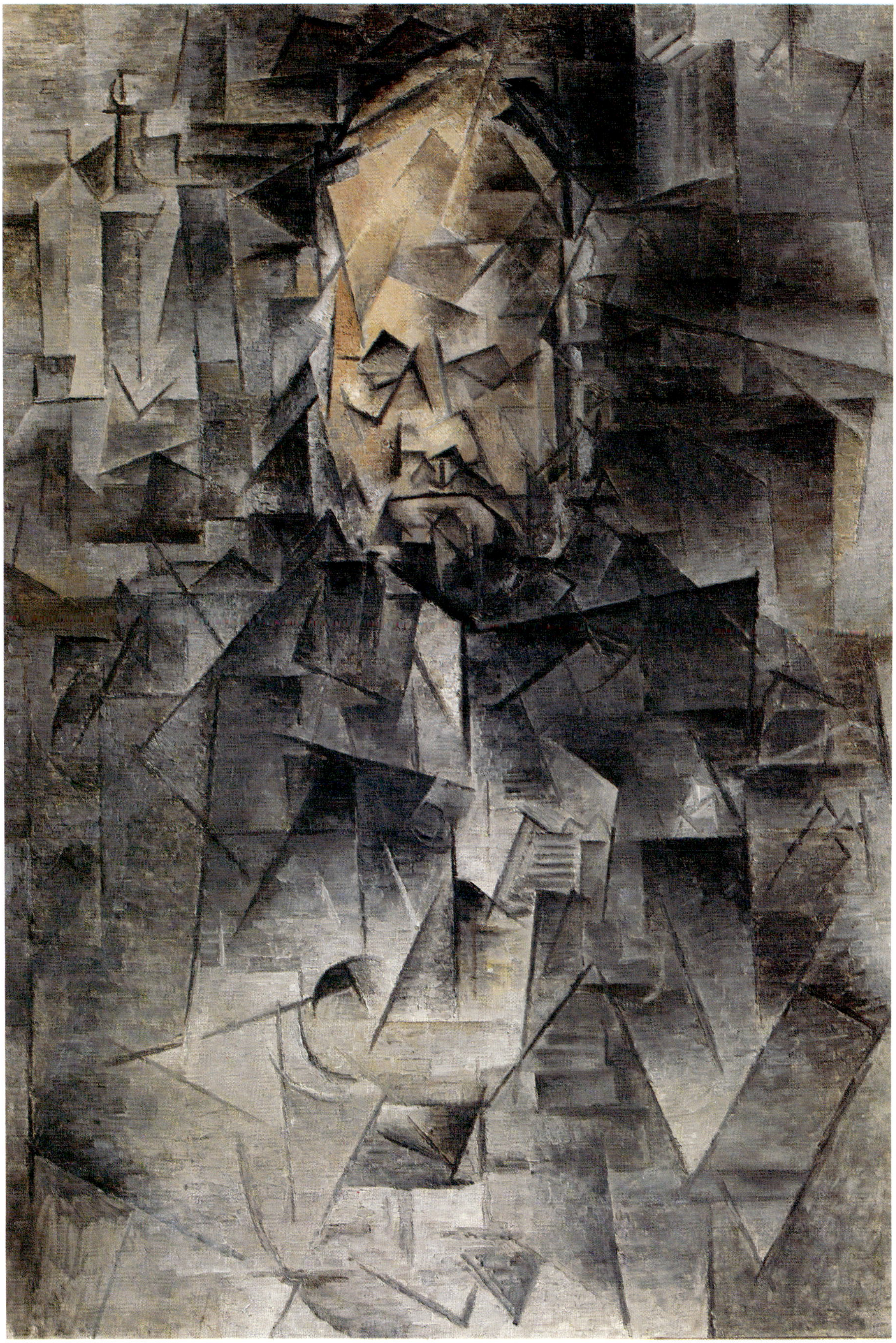

Selected Bibliography and Exhibitions

Catalogues and Handbooks

Catalogue of Paintings in the S.I. Shchukin Collection. Moscow, 1913.

S. Makovsky, "French Artists in the I.A. Morozov Collection," *Apollo*, 1913, nos. 3–4.

Catalogue of the Municipal Gallery of the Brothers Pavel and Sergei Tretyakov. Moscow, 1917.

Catalogue of the Museum of Modern Western Art. Moscow, 1928.

Louis Réau. *Catalogue of French Art in Russian Museums.* Paris, 1929.

Charles Sterling. *Hermitage Museum. French Painting from Poussin to Today.* Paris, 1957.

The Hermitage, Leningrad: French 19th-Century Masters. Introduction by A.N. Izerghina, notes by A.G. Barskaya, V.N. Berezina, A.N. Izerghina. Prague, 1968.

The Hermitage, Leningrad: French 20th-Century Masters. Introduction by A.N. Izerghina, notes by A.G. Barskaya, A.N. Izerghina, B.A. Zernov. Prague, 1970.

French Painting: Second Half of the XIX, Beginning of the XX Century from the Hermitage Museum. Introduction by A. Izerghina, editing and commentary by A. Barskaya. Leningrad, 1975.

The Hermitage: Western European Paintings of the Nineteenth and Twentieth Centuries. Introduction and notes by A. Kostenevich. Leningrad, 1976.

Hermitage Guidebook. Western European Painting: Italy, Spain, France, Switzerland. Catalogue. vol. 1, Leningrad, 1976.

Hermitage Guidebook. Western European Painting: Netherlands, Flanders, Belgium, Holland, Germany, Austria, England, Denmark, Norway, Finland, Sweden, Hungary, Poland, Rumania, Czechoslovakia. Catalogue. vol. 2, Leningrad, 1981.

A.G. Kostenevich. *French Paintings from the XIX to the Early XX Centuries in the Hermitage.* Leningrad, 1984.

Catalogues Raisonnés and Monographs

Barr

Alfred Barr. *Matisse: His Art and His Public*. New York, 1951.

Cézanne

Paul Cézanne. Introduction: A. Barskaya, notes on the plates: E. Georgievskaya and A. Barskaya.

Claude Monet

Claude Monet. Introduction: I. Sapego, authors of the catalogue: A. Barskaya and E. Georgievskaya. Leningrad, 1969.

Daix and Boudaille

P. Daix and G. Boudaille. *Picasso, 1900–1906. Catalogue Raisonné of the Paintings*. Neuchatel, 1966.

Daix and Rosselet

P. Daix and J. Rosselet. *Picasso's Cubism, 1907–1916*. Neuchatel, 1979.

Daulte

F. Daulte. *Auguste Renoir: Catalogue Raisonné of the Paintings*, vol. I. Lausanne, 1971.

De la Faille

J.B. de la Faille. *The Works of Vincent van Gogh: His Paintings and Drawings*. Amsterdam, 1970.

Matisse, 1978

Henri Matisse. *Paintings and Sculptures in Soviet Museums*. Introduction: A. Izerghina. Commentaries: A. Izerghina, A. Barskaya, T. Borovaya, E. Georgievskaya, N. Kossareva. Leningrad, 1978.

Venturi

L. Venturi. *Paul Cézanne: His Art—His Work*. Paris, 1936.

Wildenstein

G. Wildenstein. *Paul Gauguin*. Paris, 1964.

Wildenstein

G. Wildenstein. *Claude Monet: Biography and Catalogue Raisonné, Paintings*, vol. I–III. Lausanne, Paris, 1974–1979.

Zervos

Christian Zervos. *Pablo Picasso*, vol. 1–30. Paris, 1932–1975.

Exhibitions

1926 Moscow

Museum of Modern Western Art. *Paul Cézanne (1839–1906). Vincent van Gogh (1853–1890)*. Moscow, 1926.

1926 Moscow

Museum of Modern Western Art. *Paul Gauguin (1848–1903)*. Moscow, 1926.

1955 Moscow

Pushkin Museum of Fine Arts. *Exhibition of French Art from the 15th–20th Centuries*. Moscow, 1955.

1956 Moscow, Leningrad

Hermitage Museum. *Exhibition of French Art from the 12th–20th Centuries*. Moscow, Leningrad, 1956.

1956 Leningrad

Hermitage Museum. *Paul Cézanne (1839–1906), 50th Anniversary of His Death*. Leningrad, 1956.

1960 Moscow

Pushkin Museum of Fine Arts. *French Art from the Second Half of the Nineteenth Century in Russian Art Museums*. Moscow, 1960.

1965 Bordeaux

Masterpieces of French Painting in Leningrad and Moscow Museums. Bordeaux, 14 May–6 September, 1965.

1965–1966 Paris

Masterpieces of French Painting in Leningrad and Moscow Museums. Paris, Louvre, September 1965–January 1966.

1966–1967 Tokyo, Kyoto

Masterpieces of Modern Painting from the U.S.S.R.; The Hermitage, the Pushkin, the Russian, and the Tretyakov Museums in Leningrad and Moscow. Tokyo, The National Museum of Western Art, 15 October–25 December, 1966. Kyoto Municipal Museum, 14 January–28 February, 1967.

1969 Budapest

French Masterpieces from The Hermitage in Leningrad. Budapest Museum of Fine Arts, 1969.

1969 Leningrad, Moscow

Henri Matisse. Centenary. Pushkin Museum of Fine Arts and Hermitage Museum, 1969.

1971 Tokyo, Kyoto

One Hundred Masterpieces from U.S.S.R. Museums Exhibited in Japan Under Auspices of the Tokyo National Museum. April 10–May 30, 1971. Kyoto National Museum, June 8–July 25, 1971.

1971 Paris

Picasso in Soviet Museums. Paris, Museum of Modern Art, 1971.

1972 Otterlo

From van Gogh to Picasso: Nineteenth- and Twentieth-Century Paintings and Drawings from the Pushkin Museum and the Hermitage in Leningrad. Otterlo, Kröller-Müller Museum, April 30–July 16, 1972.

1972 Leningrad

Portrait Painting from the Collection of the Hermitage Museum in Leningrad: Ancient Egypt, Eastern and Western Europe. Leningrad, 1972.

1973 Washington, New York, Chicago, Detroit, Ft. Worth, Los Angeles

Impressionist and Post-Impressionist Paintings from the U.S.S.R. lent by The Hermitage Museum, Leningrad, The Pushkin Museum, Moscow. National Gallery of Art, Washington, D.C.; M. Knoedler and Co., Inc., New York; Los Angeles County Museum of Art; The Art Institute of Chicago, Chicago; The Kimbell Art Museum, Fort Worth, Texas; The Institute of Arts, Detroit, 1973.

1974 Leningrad, 1975 Moscow

Impressionist Painting: 100th Anniversary of the First Impressionist Exhibition in 1874. Hermitage Museum, Leningrad, and Pushkin Museum, Moscow, 1974 and 1975.

1979 Tokyo, Kyoto, Kamakura

Exhibition of Works by French Artists from the End of the 19th to the Beginning of the 20th Centuries from the Collection of the Hermitage Museum and the Pushkin Museum. The Municipal Museum, Tokyo; The Museum of Modern Art, Kyoto; The Museum of Modern Art of the Prefecture of Kanagawa, Kamakura, 1979.

1982 Leningrad

Pablo Picasso, 1881–1973. Exhibition on the Occasion of the Centenary of the Artist's Birth. Leningrad, 1982.

1983 Lugano

Impressionist and Post-Impressionist Paintings from Soviet Museums. Lugano, Thyssen-Bornemisza Collection, Villa Favorita, 1983.

1985 Venice, Rome

Cézanne, Monet, Renoir, Gauguin, van Gogh, Matisse, Picasso: 42 Paintings from Soviet Museums. Venice, Correr Museum. Rome, Capitoline Museum, 1985.